HARCOURT SCIENCE

TEACHING RESOURCES

Harcourt School Publishers

Orlando • Boston • Dallas • Chicago • San Diego

www.harcourtschool.com

ISBN 0-15-324477-1

5 6 7 8 9 10   082   10 09 08 07 06 05 04

HARCOURT SCIENCE
Contents

School-Home Connections — TR1–26

Unit A, Chapter 1	Living and Nonliving Things	TR1
Unit A, Chapter 2	All About Plants	TR3
Unit A, Chapter 3	All About Animals	TR5
Unit B, Chapter 1	Plants and Animals Need One Another	TR7
Unit B, Chapter 2	A Place to Live	TR9
Unit C, Chapter 1	Earth's Land	TR11
Unit C, Chapter 2	Our Natural Resources	TR13
Unit D, Chapter 1	Measuring Weather	TR15
Unit D, Chapter 2	The Sky and The Seasons	TR17
Unit E, Chapter 1	Investigate Matter	TR19
Unit E, Chapter 2	Making Sound	TR21
Unit F, Chapter 1	Pushes and Pulls	TR23
Unit F, Chapter 2	Magnets	TR25

Investigate Logs — TR27–79

Participating in a School Science Fair — TR80–85

Picture Cards — TR86–97

Activities for Home or School — TR98–109

Vocabulary Activities — TR110–116

Vocabulary Cards — TR117–160

Investigate Data Charts — TR161–168

Harcourt

Maps, Charts, Patterns, Graphs TR169–179

Project Planning Chart TR168
Pattern Cutouts TR169
Pop-up Book Pattern TR170
Booklet Cover Pattern TR171
Seasons Pattern Cutout TR172
Butterfly Pattern TR173
Flowchart TR174
Venn Diagram TR175
K-W-L Chart TR176
Web Organizer TR177
Chart Organizer TR178
1-in. Grid Paper TR179

Writing in Science TR181–186

Model: Information Sentences TR182
Model: Paragraph That Describes TR183
Model: How-To Sentences TR184
Model: Story TR185
Model: Letter TR186

Harcourt

 # School-Home Connection

Chapter Content

Today we begin a new chapter in science. Your child will be learning about living and non-living things. We will be doing science activities that use the senses to help learn about the things around us. We will also observe and learn about the characteristics of living and nonliving things.

Science Process Skills

Learning to **observe** carefully is one of the most important skills of science. Observing is more than looking with the eyes. The senses of smell, hearing, touch, and sometimes taste also play a part in making careful observations.

To encourage the ability to observe carefully and accurately, together walk around your home and choose one thing for your child to observe closely in each room. Encourage your child to use as many senses as possible to describe the things he or she observes.

Science Fun

Children's books can provide fun science connections, as they often have science ideas woven into their stories. Pointing these connections out helps children see that science is part of life both inside and outside the classroom.

Animals and Their World by Sally Morgan (Young Discoverers: Biology Facts and Experiments Series, 1996).

Your child may enjoy learning about how animals use their senses in *Animals and Their World* by Sally Morgan. This book contains many activities in addition to providing information about how animals use their senses to hunt for food, protect themselves, and communicate with one another.

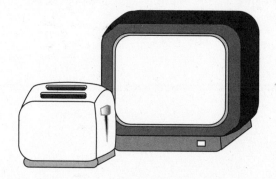

Activity Materials from Home

Dear Family Member:

To do the activities in this chapter, we will need some materials that you may have around the house. Look at the items listed at the right. If possible, please send these things to school with your child.

Your help and support are appreciated!

____ **piece of fruit**
____ **small rocks**

Harcourt

La escuela y la casa

Contenido del capítulo

Hoy comenzamos un nuevo capítulo de ciencias. Su hijo(a) aprenderá sobre los seres vivos y no vivos. Realizaremos actividades científicas usando los sentidos para aprender sobre las cosas que nos rodean. También observaremos y aprenderemos las características de los seres vivos y no vivos.

Destrezas del proceso científico

Aprender a **observar** detalladamente es una de las destrezas más importantes de las ciencias. Observar es más que mirar con los ojos. Los sentidos del olfato, la audición, el tacto y algunas veces del gusto también contribuyen a hacer observaciones detalladas.

Para estimular la habilidad de observar detalladamente y con precisión, camine con su hijo(a) por su casa y elija algo para que él (ella) lo observe en detalle en cada habitación. Anímelo(a) a que use tantos sentidos como sea posible al describir las cosas que observa.

Diversión

Los libros infantiles pueden proporcionar conexiones de ciencias divertidas, ya que a menudo sus historias contienen ideas científicas. Señalar estas conexiones ayuda a los niños a comprender que las ciencias forman parte de la vida dentro y fuera del salón de clases.

Animals and Their World de Sally Morgan (Young Discoverers: Biology Facts and Experiments Series, 1996).

Quizás su hijo(a) se divierta aprendiendo cómo los animales usan sus sentidos en *Animals and Their World* de Sally Morgan. Este libro contiene muchas actividades además de proporcionar información de cómo los animales usan sus sentidos para cazar, protegerse y comunicarse con los demás.

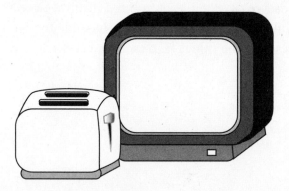

Materiales de casa para la actividad

Querido familiar:

Para hacer las actividades de este capítulo, necesitaremos algunos materiales que tal vez tenga en la casa. Observe los artículos de la lista de la derecha. Si es posible, por favor envíe estas cosas con su hijo(a) a la escuela.

¡Gracias por su ayuda y su apoyo!

_____ **fruta**
_____ **rocas pequeñas**

Harcourt

School-Home Connection

Chapter Content

Today in science we began a chapter on plants. We will be doing science activities that identify the parts of a plant, how a plant grows, and what a plant needs to live and grow.

Science Process Skills

Learning to **observe** carefully is one of the most important skills in science. By observing carefully and keeping careful records of what was observed, scientists can remember what they have done during an experiment and draw conclusions about what they have observed.

Help your child observe and record the changes that the seed in **Science Fun** undergoes as it grows into a mature plant. Encourage your child to draw the seed and resulting plant every few days. Help him or her record how much water is given, measure the height of the plant, and so on.

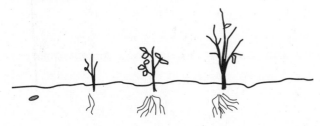

Science Fun

With your child, select and grow an indoor or outdoor plant from seed. You might choose an ornamental plant, such as a coleus, or a garden plant, such as parsley or beans.

What You Need

- seeds
- water
- potting soil
- container such as a paper cup

What to Do

1. Fill the cup three-fourths full of soil. Be sure the soil is damp, but not wet.

2. Plant the seeds by following package directions.

3. Place the cup in a sunny window or in a well-lighted area.

4. Keep a record of all the things you and your child do to care for the plant. Be sure not to over-water your plant.

Activity Materials from Home

Dear Family Member:

To do the activities in this chapter, we will need some materials that you may have around the house. Look at the items listed at the right. If possible, please send these things to school with your child.

Your help and support are appreciated!

____ **carrot with leafy top**
____ **unsharpened pencil**

La escuela y la casa

Contenido del capítulo

Hoy comenzamos un nuevo capítulo de ciencias. Su hijo(a) aprenderá sobre las plantas. Realizaremos actividades científicas que identifican las partes de una planta, cómo crece una planta y qué necesita una planta para vivir y crecer.

Destrezas del proceso científico

Aprender a **observar** detalladamente es una de las destrezas más importantes de las ciencias. Al observar detalladamente y anotar con cuidado lo que se ha observado, los científicos pueden recordar lo que han hecho durante un experimento y sacar conclusiones sobre de lo que han observado.

Ayude a su hijo(a) a observar y anotar los cambios que sufre la semilla en **Diversión** a medida que crece y se convierte en una planta madura. Anime a su hijo(a) a dibujar la semilla y la planta a medida que crece cada dos o tres días. Ayúdelo a anotar cuánta agua se le da, medir la altura de la planta y así sucesivamente.

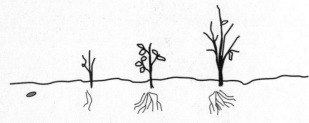

Diversión

Con su hijo(a), seleccione y cultive una semilla de una planta de interior o exterior. Quizás elija una planta ornamental como un coleo o una planta de jardín como perejil o frijoles.

Lo que necesitas

- semillas
- agua
- tierra para plantar
- recipiente como un vaso de papel

Lo que vas a hacer

1. Llena el vaso con tres cuartos de tierra. Asegúrate de que la tierra esté húmeda, pero no empapada.

2. Siembra las semillas siguiendo las instrucciones del paquete.

3. Coloca el vaso en una ventana donde le dé el sol o en un área bien iluminada.

4. Anote todas las cosas que Ud. y su hijo(a) hacen para cuidar la planta. Asegúrese de que no le echen mucha agua a la planta.

Materiales de casa para la actividad

Querido familiar:

Para hacer las actividades en este capítulo, necesitaremos algunos materiales que tal vez tenga en la casa. Observe los artículos de la lista de la derecha. Si es posible, por favor envíe estas cosas con su hijo(a) a la escuela.

____ **zanahoria con el tope frondoso**
____ **lápiz sin punta**

¡Gracias por su ayuda y su apoyo!

Harcourt

School-Home Connection

Chapter Content

Today we begin a new chapter in science. Your child will be learning about different kinds of animals, what their needs are, and how some kinds of animals grow. We will be doing science activities such as observing animals and making model animals.

Science Process Skills

Just as students learn to sequence events in math, they learn to **sequence** the steps of a process in science. The life stages of plants and animals lend themselves to the reinforcement of this skill.

With your child, select an animal to study. Learn about the animal's life cycle, where it lives, and what things it needs to survive. Help your child draw pictures of the animal at different stages of its life. Mix up the pictures, and let your child sequence them from young animal to adult. Encourage your child to tell you how the animal has changed in each picture.

Science Fun

Children's books can provide fun science connections, as they often have science ideas woven into their stories. Pointing out these connections helps children see that science is part of life both inside and outside the classroom.

Animals on the Move by Allan Fowler (Children's Press, 2000).

Your child may enjoy reading this exciting book about animal migration. The migration patterns of fish, mammals, birds, and butterflies are discussed. Encourage your child to pick one kind of animal and do further research on its migration habits.

Activity Materials from Home

Dear Family Member:

To do the activities in this chapter, we will need some materials that you may have around the house. Look at the items listed at the right. If possible, please send these things to school with your child.

Your help and support are appreciated!

____ **leaves on a twig**
____ **small rocks and twigs**
____ **bottle cap**
____ **toothpicks**
____ **wax paper**

La escuela y la casa

Harcourt Ciencias

Contenido del capítulo

Hoy comenzamos un nuevo capítulo de ciencias. Su hijo(a) aprenderá sobre los diferentes tipos de animales, cuáles son sus necesidades y cómo crecen ciertos tipos de animales. Realizaremos actividades científicas como observar los animales y hacer modelos de animales.

Destrezas del proceso científico

Así como los estudiantes aprenden a ordenar los sucesos en matemáticas, también aprenden la **secuencia** de los pasos en un proceso científico. Las etapas de la vida de las plantas y los animales les permiten reforzar esta destreza.

Con su hijo(a), seleccione un animal para estudiarlo. Aprenda sobre los ciclos de vida del animal, dónde vive y cuáles son las cosas que necesita para sobrevivir. Ayude a su hijo(a) a hacer dibujos de un animal en las diferentes etapas de su vida. Mezcle las ilustraciones y deje que su hijo(a) las coloque en **secuencia** desde un animal joven hasta un adulto. Anímelo(a) a decir cómo ha cambiado el animal en cada dibujo.

Diversión

Los libros infantiles pueden proporcionar conexiones de ciencias divertidas, ya que a menudo sus historias contienen ideas científicas. Señalar estas conexiones ayuda a los niños a comprender que las ciencias forman parte de la vida dentro y fuera del salón de clases.

Animals on the Move de Allan Fowler (Children's Press, 2000).

Quizás su hijo(a) disfrute leyendo este libro interesante sobre la migración de los animales. El libro trata sobre los patrones de las migraciones de peces, mamíferos, aves y mariposas.

Anime a su hijo(a) a elegir un tipo de animal y a investigar sobre sus hábitos de migración.

Materiales de casa para la actividad

Querido familiar:

Para hacer las actividades en este capítulo, necesitaremos algunos materiales que tal vez tenga en la casa. Observe los artículos de la lista de la derecha. Si es posible, por favor envíe estas cosas con su hijo(a) a la escuela.

¡Gracias por su ayuda y su apoyo!

____ hojas en una ramita
____ rocas pequeñas y ramitas
____ tapa de una botella
____ palillos de dientes
____ papel encerado

School-Home Connection

Harcourt Science

Chapter Content

Today we begin a new chapter in science. Your child will be learning about how animals use plants to meet their needs as well as how animals can help plants. We will also study how people use both plants and animals to meet their needs. We will be doing science activities that study different ways animals use plants, how animals help plants, and different ways people use plants and animals.

Science Process Skills

Learning to **classify** objects or events into categories is an important skill in science. By placing things into similar groups, scientists can make generalizations about how the world works or how things are related to one another.

With your child walk around your home. After observing a number of objects, decide on two groups into which you could sort the items. For example, you might sort items into those made of plastic and those not made of plastic, or those that use electricity and those that don't. As your child studies the information in this chapter, he or she will learn that this sorting process is one step in classifying things.

Science Fun

Children's books can provide fun science connections, as they often have science ideas woven into their stories. Pointing these connections out helps children see that science is part of life both inside and outside the classroom.

Warm as Wool by Scott Russell Sanders (Simon & Schuster, 1998).

Your child may enjoy reading *Warm as Wool* by Scott Russell Sanders. The story is set in 1804 as a family moves across country. Once in their new home, Betsy Ward, the mother, buys a flock of sheep. She then spins cloth and makes clothes from the wool in order to keep her family warm during the winter.

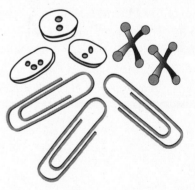

Activity Materials from Home

Dear Family Member:

To do the activities in this chapter, we will need some materials that you may have around the house. Look at the items listed at the right. If possible, please send these things to school with your child.

Your help and support are appreciated!

____ **string or yarn**
____ **Velcro**
____ **cotton balls**
____ **sandpaper**
____ **Styrofoam balls**

Harcourt

La escuela y la casa

Harcourt Ciencias

Contenido del capítulo

Hoy comenzamos un nuevo capítulo de ciencias. Su hijo(a) aprenderá sobre cómo las personas, los animales y las plantas se necesitan unas a otras. Realizaremos actividades científicas que estudian las diferentes formas en que los animales usan las plantas, cómo los animales ayudan a las plantas y las diferentes formas en que las personas usan las plantas y los animales.

Destrezas del proceso científico

Aprender a **clasificar** objetos o sucesos en categorías es una destreza importante de las ciencias. Al colocar cosas en grupos iguales, los científicos pueden hacer generalizaciones sobre cómo trabaja el mundo o cómo se relacionan las cosas entre sí.

Camine con su hijo(a) por su casa. Después de observar un número de objetos, decida en dos grupos en los cuales podría ordenar los artículos. Por ejemplo, quizás quiera ordenar lo artículos en los que son de plástico y los que no son de plástico o los que usan electricidad y los que no. Mientras su hijo(a) estudia la información en este capítulo, él aprenderá que este proceso de clasificación es un paso para ordenar las cosas.

Diversión

Los libros infantiles pueden proporcionar conexiones de ciencias divertidas, ya que a menudo sus historias contienen ideas científicas. Señalar estas conexiones ayuda a los niños a comprender que las ciencias forman parte de la vida dentro y fuera del salón de clases.

Warm as Wool de Scott Russell Sanders (Simon & Schuster, 1998).

Quizás su hijo(a) se divierta leyendo *Warm as Wool* de Scott Russell Sanders. La historia ocurre en 1804 a medida que una familia se movilizaba por el país. Una vez que estaban en su nuevo hogar, Betsy Ward, la madre, compra un rebaño de ovejas. Después hila y hace ropa de la lana para poder mantener a su familia abrigada durante el invierno.

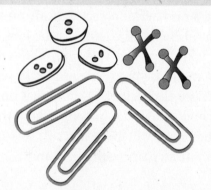

Materiales de casa para la actividad

Querido familiar:

Para hacer las actividades en este capítulo, necesitaremos algunos materiales que tal vez tenga en la casa. Observe los artículos de la lista de la derecha. Si es posible, por favor envíe estas cosas con su hijo(a) a la escuela.

¡Gracias por su ayuda y su apoyo!

____ **hilo o estambre**
____ **Velcro**
____ **bolitas de algodón**
____ **papel de lija**
____ **bolitas de estireno**

Harcourt

School-Home Connection

Harcourt Science

Chapter Content

Today in science we began studying about where plants and animals live. Your child will be learning about living things in a forest, desert, rain forest, and ocean. We will be doing science activities that help us study the different kinds of plants and animals that live in these places.

Science Process Skills

Learning to **draw conclusions** is an important skill of science. Students not only need to draw conclusions from the activities they do, but also from the materials they read.

Go to the library together and read *The Great Kapok Tree: A Tale of the Amazon Rain Forest* (Harcourt Brace, 1998). In this story, a man is set to cut down a great kapok tree that is home to a variety of animals. These animals try to persuade the man not to destroy their home. Help your child draw a conclusion as to what would happen to the animals in the forest if the tree were to be cut down.

Science Fun

Make a mini-terrarium out of a two-liter soft drink bottle.

What You Need

- scissors
- potting soil
- spoon
- several small plants
- clean 2-L bottle
- clean gravel
- water
- plastic wrap
- rubber band

What to Do

1. Carefully cut off the top of the 2-L bottle.
2. Help your child make a thin layer of gravel, followed by a thicker layer of soil, in the bottom of the bottle.
3. Use the spoon to gently place the plants in the soil. Press the plants firmly in place.
4. Water the plants well.
5. Cover the top of the bottle with plastic wrap and secure with a rubber band.
6. Observe the terrarium for several weeks and record what you observe.

Activity Materials from Home

Dear Family Member:

To do the activities in this chapter, we will need some materials that you may have around the house. Look at the items listed at the right. If possible, please send these things to school with your child.

Your help and support are appreciated!

____ **paper towels**
____ **wax paper**
____ **alfalfa seeds**
____ **cotton balls**
____ **plastic film canisters**

Harcourt

La escuela y la casa

Contenido del capítulo

Hoy comenzamos un nuevo capítulo de ciencias. Su hijo(a) aprenderá sobre los seres vivos del bosque, del desierto, del bosque tropical y del océano. Realizaremos actividades científicas que nos ayudarán a estudiar los diferentes tipos de plantas y animales que viven en estos lugares.

Destrezas del proceso científico

Aprender a **sacar conclusiones** es una destreza importante de las ciencias. Los estudiantes no sólo necesitan sacar conclusiones de las actividades que hacen sino también de los materiales que leen.

Vayan a la biblioteca y lean *The Great Kapok Tree: A Tale of the Amazon Rain Forest* (Harcourt Brace, 1998). En esta historia un hombre quiere cortar un miraguano que es el hogar de una serie de animales. Estos animales tratan de persuadir al hombre a no destruir su hogar. Ayude a su hijo(a) a sacar una conclusión de lo que les pasaría a los animales del bosque si se talara el árbol.

Diversión

Hacer un terrario en miniatura de una botella de refresco.

Lo que necesitas

- tijeras
- tierra para plantar
- cuchara
- algunas plantas pequeñas
- botella limpia de 2L
- gravilla limpia
- agua
- papel de plástico
- elástico

Lo que vas a hacer

1. Corta con cuidado el borde superior de la botella de 2L.

2. Ayude a su hijo(a) a hacer una capa de gravilla delgada, seguida de una capa más gruesa de tierra en el fondo de la botella.

3. Usa la cuchara para colocar suavemente las plantas en la tierra. Presiona las plantas con firmeza en el lugar.

4. Riega bien las plantas.

5. Cubre la parte superior de la botella con papel de plástico y asegúrela con un elástico.

6. Observa el terrario por algunas semanas y anota lo que observas.

Materiales de casa para la actividad

Querido familiar:

Para hacer las actividades en este capítulo, necesitaremos algunos materiales que tal vez tenga en la casa. Observe los artículos de la lista de la derecha. Si es posible, por favor envíe estas cosas con su hijo(a) a la escuela.

¡Gracias por su ayuda y su apoyo!

_____ **toallas de papel**
_____ **papel encerado**
_____ **semillas de alfalfa**
_____ **bolitas de algodón**
_____ **recipientes de plástico de rollos de películas**

Harcourt

School-Home Connection

Chapter Content

Today we begin a new chapter in science. Your child will be learning about Earth's land. We will be doing science activities that include observing rocks and comparing different kinds of fossils.

Science Process Skills

Learning to **observe** carefully is an important science skill. This activity will help your child develop his or her ability to observe.

Gather a few leaves from outside and some blank sheets of paper and crayons. Have your child place a piece of paper over each leaf and make a rubbing with a crayon. After your child has finished rubbing each leaf pattern, have her or him compare the actual leaf to the rubbing. Then discuss how the pattern of the leaf on the paper resembles the imprint that some fossils leave in rocks.

Science Fun

Scientists study fossils to learn about what life was like a long time ago. You and your child can work together to predict what future scientists will say about our time.

What You Need

- index cards
- pencil
- crayons

What to Do

1. Have your child use crayons to draw pictures on index cards showing objects that represent our current time.

2. Have your child write on the back of each card with a pencil, describing how the object tells about our world.

3. Have your child predict which of these things might be studied by scientists 500 years from now.

Activity Materials from Home

Dear Family Member:

To do the activities in this chapter, we will need some materials that you may have around the house. Please note the items at the right. If possible, please send these things to school with your child.

Your help and support are appreciated!

____ **small rocks**
____ **petroleum jelly**

Harcourt

La escuela y la casa

Contenido del capítulo

Hoy comenzamos un capítulo nuevo en nuestra clase de ciencias. Su niño(a) aprenderá acerca del suelo en la Tierra. Realizaremos actividades de ciencias tales como observar rocas y comparar diferentes clases de fósiles.

Destrezas del proceso científico

Aprender a **observar** cuidadosamente es una destreza importante para ciencias. Esta actividad ayudará a su niño(a) a desarrollar la habilidad de observar.

Necesitarán algunas hojas de árboles y algunas hojas en blanco y creyones. Pida a su niño(a) que ponga una hoja de papel sobre cada hoja de árbol y que con el creyón las calque. Después comente cómo el patrón de las hojas de árbol en el calco se asemeja a las marcas que algunos fósiles dejan en las rocas.

Diversión

Los científicos estudian los fósiles para aprender acerca de cómo era la vida hace mucho tiempo. Ud. y su niño(a) pueden trabajar juntos para hacer una predicción de lo que creen que los científicos del futuro dirán acerca de nuestros tiempos.

Lo que necesitas
- tarjetas
- lápiz
- creyones

Lo que vas a hacer

1. Pida a su niño(a) que en las tarjetas con un creyón haga dibujos que muestren objetos de la época actual.

2. Invite a su niño a que en la parte posterior de cada tarjeta, escriba con un lápiz una descripción de cómo el objeto nos dice algo de nuestra época.

3. Pida a su niño que haga una predicción acerca de cuál de estos objetos pudiera ser estudiado por los científicos dentro de 500 años.

Materiales de casa para la actividad

Querido familiar:

Para hacer las actividades en este capítulo, necesitaremos algunos materiales que tal vez tenga en la casa. Observe los artículos de la lista de la derecha. Si es posible, por favor envíe estas cosas con su hijo(a) a la escuela.

¡Gracias por su ayuda y su apoyo!

_____ rocas pequeñas
_____ vaselina

Harcourt

School-Home Connection

Harcourt Science

Chapter Content

Today we begin a new chapter in science. Your child will be learning about Earth's air and water. We will be doing science activities that investigate the air around us. We will also learn about where fresh water is found on Earth.

Science Process Skills

Learning to **communicate** is an important skill in science. By communicating through words or drawings, children can convey the results of a science activity.

Use the picture you and your child draw as the conclusion to **Science Fun** as a writing prompt. Have your child think of two or three words that describe a waterless day. Children might suggest words such as dry, thirsty, or dusty. Help your child write sentences for each word he or she lists.

Science Fun

Everyone uses water every day. This activity will help your child understand how much we depend on this important resource.

Talk with your child about how your family uses water. Make a list of all the things you can think of. The list might include bathing, cooking, drinking, cleaning, brushing teeth, flushing toilets, and so on. Encourage your child to think of less obvious ways water is used, such as to grow the plants and animals we use for food.

When the list is complete, have your child think about a day without water. Work together to draw a picture of what this day would be like.

Activity Materials from Home

Dear Family Member:

To do the activities in this chapter, we will need some materials that you may have around the house. Please note the items listed at the right. If possible, please send these things to school with your child.

Your help and support are appreciated!

____ **plastic produce bag**
____ **plastic spoons**
____ **plastic wrap**
____ **small marbles**
____ **salt**
____ **aluminum foil**
____ **newspaper**

La escuela y la casa

Harcourt Ciencias

Contenido del capítulo

Hoy comenzamos un nuevo capítulo de ciencias. Su hijo(a) aprenderá sobre el aire y el agua de la Tierra. Realizaremos actividades científicas que investigan el aire que nos rodea. También aprenderemos dónde se halla el agua dulce en la Tierra.

Destrezas del proceso científico

Aprender a **comunicar** es una destreza importante de las ciencias. Al comunicarse a través de las palabras o ilustraciones, los niños pueden expresar los resultados de una actividad científica.

Usen el dibujo que Ud. y su hijo(a) hicieron en la conclusión de **Diversión** como una sugerencia para hacer la descripción por escrito. Pida a su hijo(a) que piense en dos o tres palabras que describan un día sin agua. Los niños podrían sugerir palabras como seco, sediento o polvoriento. Ayude a su hijo(a) a escribir oraciones para cada palabra que enumere.

Diversión

Todo el mundo usa el agua todos los días. Esta actividad ayudará a su hijo(a) a comprender cuánto dependemos de este importante recurso.

Hable con su hijo(a) sobre cómo su familia usa el agua. Elabore una lista de todas las cosas en las que puede pensar. La lista debe incluir bañarse, cocinar, beber, limpiar, cepillarse los dientes, bajar la palanca del baño y así sucesivamente. Anime a su hijo(a) para que piense en las maneras menos obvias en que se usa el agua como cultivar las plantas y criar los animales que usamos como alimento.

Cuando la lista esté completa, pida a su hijo(a) que piense sobre un día sin agua. Trabajen para elaborar un dibujo de cómo sería ese día.

Materiales de casa para la actividad

Querido familiar:

Para hacer las actividades de este capítulo, necesitaremos algunos materiales que tal vez tenga en la casa. Observe los artículos de la lista de la derecha. Si es posible, por favor envíe estas cosas con su hijo(a) a la escuela.

¡Gracias por su ayuda y su apoyo!

____ **bolsa de plástico**
____ **cucharas de plástico**
____ **papel de plástico**
____ **canicas pequeñas**
____ **sal**
____ **papel de aluminio**
____ **periódico**

School-Home Connection

Chapter Content

Today we begin a new chapter in science. Your child will be learning about the weather. We will be doing activities that investigate sky conditions, measure temperature, observe wind direction, and find out how clouds are formed.

Science Process Skills

Learning to **compare** is an important skill of science. Children are asked to identify common and distinguishing characteristics among objects or events.

To encourage the ability to compare, help your child observe the weather for one week. Record your observations at the end of each day. Compare how each day's weather is similar to or different from the last. Encourage your child to use comparison words such as warmer, cooler, windier, wetter, and so on.

Science Fun

Make a decorative wind sock to hang outdoors. Your child can use the sock to observe the wind.

You Will Need

- large sheet of tissue paper or light cloth
- long, thin strips of tissue paper
- several chenille sticks   • tape
- string or yarn   • scissors

What to Do

1. Roll the large sheet of tissue paper into a tube that has a 4-in. diameter. Secure with tape.

2. Use chenille sticks to form two rings that are the same size as the diameter of the tube. Attach one ring to one end of the tube with tape.

3. Attach the tissue strips around one end of the tube so they hang freely.

4. Cut three 3-in. pieces of string. Tape the pieces equidistant around the top of the tube. Tie the free ends of the strings together. Add a longer piece of string for hanging. Hang.

Activity Materials from Home

Dear Family Member:

To do the activities in this chapter, we will need some materials that you may have around the house. Please note the items at the right. If possible, please send these things to school with your child.

Your help and support are appreciated!

_____ **drinking straws**
_____ **toothpicks**

Harcourt

La escuela y la casa

Harcourt Ciencias

Contenido del capítulo

Hoy comenzamos un nuevo capítulo de ciencias. Su hijo(a) aprenderá sobre el clima. Realizaremos actividades científicas que investigan las condiciones del cielo, medir la temperatura, observar la dirección del viento y descubrir cómo se forman las nubes.

Destrezas del proceso científico

Aprender a **comparar** es una destreza importante de ciencias. A los niños se les pide que identifiquen características comunes y distintivas entre objetos o sucesos.

Para estimular la habilidad de comparar, ayude a su hijo(a) a observar el clima por una semana. Anote sus observaciones al final de cada día. Compare cómo el clima de cada día se parece o se diferencia al del día anterior. Anime a su hijo(a) para que use palabras de comparación como más caliente, más frío, más húmedo y otras.

Diversión

Hacer una manga de aire para colgarla afuera. Su hijo(a) puede usar la manga para observar el viento.

Lo que necesitas

- hoja grande de papel de seda o tela suave
- tiras largas y delgadas de papel de seda
- algunos palitos de felpilla • cinta adhesiva
- hilo o estambre • tijeras

Lo que vas a hacer

1. Enrolla la hoja grande de papel de seda en un tubo que tenga un diámetro de 4 pulg. Asegúralo con la cinta adhesiva.

2. Usa los palitos de felpilla para formar dos anillos que sean del mismo tamaño del diámetro del tubo. Amarra un anillo a uno de los extremos del tubo con cinta adhesiva.

3. Amarra las tiras de papel de seda alrededor de uno de los extremos del tubo de manera que cuelguen libremente.

4. Corta tres pedazos de hilo de 3 pulg. Pega los pedazos a igual distancia alrededor de la punta del tubo. Amarra juntos los extremos libres de los hilos. Agrega un pedazo más largo de hilo para que cuelgue. Cuelga la manga.

Materiales de casa para la actividad

Querido familiar:

Para hacer las actividades de este capítulo, necesitaremos algunos materiales que tal vez tenga en la casa. Observe los artículos de la lista de la derecha. Si es posible, por favor envíe estas cosas con su hijo(a) a la escuela.

_____ **pajitas de beber**
_____ **palillos de dientes**

¡Gracias por su ayuda y su apoyo!

Harcourt

School-Home Connection

Harcourt Science

Chapter Content

Today we begin a new chapter in science. Your child will be learning about the sky and the seasons. We will be doing science activities that investigate the best season to sprout seeds, colors and fabrics that help to keep children cool and warm in different seasons, and how some animals store food for the winter. We will also investigate what we can see in the sky.

Science Process Skills

Learning to **predict** is an important skill of science. A scientific prediction is made once a pattern has been observed. Children are asked to think about previous observations before making predictions.

Show your child a seed. Have your child use past observations to predict the stages the plant will go through as it grows from a seed to a mature plant. Talk about how different climates might affect the growth of the plant. If possible, plant the seed and compare its growth to the predictions you made together.

ScienceFun

Help your child select a part of the country or world with seasonal changes different from those you experience in your area. Use library resources to find out about the climate in the area you chose. Your child may wish to make a collage or poster showing what people do differently there because of the climate.

Dear Rebecca, Winter is Here by Jean Craighead George (Harpercollins Juvenile Books, 1993).

Your child may enjoy learning about the changing seasons in *Dear Rebecca, Winter is Here*, by Jean Craighead George. In this story, an elderly woman writes to her granddaughter about the changes that take place in nature when winter comes.

Activity Materials from Home

Dear Family Member:

To do the activities in this chapter, we will need some materials that you may have around the house. Please note the items listed at the right. If possible, please send these things to school with your child.

Your help and support are appreciated!

____ **apples**
____ **string**
____ **zip-top bags**
____ **scraps of wool**
____ **cotton balls**
____ **Styrofoam "peanuts"**
____ **newspaper**

La escuela y la casa

Contenido del capítulo

Hoy comenzamos un nuevo capítulo de ciencias. Su hijo(a) aprenderá sobre el cielo y las estaciones del año. Realizaremos actividades científicas que investigan la mejor temporada para que broten las semillas, los colores y las telas que ayudan a los niños a mantenerse frescos y cálidos en temporadas diferentes y cómo algunos animales guardan comida en el invierno. También investigaremos lo que podemos ver en el cielo.

Destrezas del proceso científico

Aprender a **predecir** es una destreza importante de las ciencias. Una predicción científica se realiza una vez que se ha observado un patrón. A los niños se les pide que piensen sobre observaciones previas antes de hacer predicciones.

Muéstrele a su hijo(a) una semilla. Pida a su hijo(a) que use las observaciones pasadas para predecir las etapas por la que pasará la planta a medida que se convierte de una semilla hasta una planta madura. Hable sobre cómo los diferentes climas podrían afectar el crecimiento de la planta. Si es posible, siembre la semilla y compare su crecimiento con las predicciones que hicieron juntos.

Diversión

Ayude a su hijo(a) a seleccionar una parte del país o del mundo con diferentes cambios de estaciones como las que ha experimentado en su área. Use los recursos de la biblioteca para descubrir los climas en el área que eligió. Su hijo(a) quizás desee hacer un collage o cartel que muestre lo que hacen las personas diferente allí debido al clima.

Dear Rebecca, Winter is Here de Jean Craighead George (Harpercollins Juvenile Books, 1993).

Quizás su hijo(a) se divierta aprendiendo sobre las estaciones del año en *Dear Rebecca, Winter is Here* de Jean Craighead George. En esta historia, una mujer mayor le escribe a su nieta sobre los cambios que suceden en la naturaleza cuando llega el invierno.

Materiales de casa para la actividad

Querido familiar:

Para hacer las actividades en este capítulo, necesitaremos algunos materiales que tal vez tenga en la casa. Observe los artículos de la lista de la derecha. Si es posible, por favor envíe estas cosas con su hijo(a) a la escuela.

¡Gracias por su ayuda y su apoyo!

_____ **manzanas**
_____ **hilo**
_____ **bolsas de plástico con cierre**
_____ **pedacitos de lana**
_____ **bolitas de algodón**
_____ **bolitas de espuma de estireno**
_____ **periódico**

School-Home Connection

Chapter Content

Today we begin a new chapter in science about matter. Your child will be learning about solids, liquids, and gases. We will do activities that explore the properties of solids, liquids, and gases. We will also investigate what makes objects float or sink. We will finish the chapter by learning how we can change matter.

Science Process Skills

Learning to **gather and record data** is an important skill in science. To encourage your child to practice gathering and recording data, find objects around the house that can either sink or float. Sinking and floating are physical properties of matter. Have your child predict whether each object will sink or float. Help your child record his or her predictions. Then test the objects and record what you observed. Help your child understand that recording data makes it easier to remember what has happened and talk about observations with others. It also aids in drawing conclusions about what has been observed.

Science Fun

Matter has different physical properties.

Candy Creatures

What You Need

- assorted candies, gum drops, chocolate chips, marshmallows, licorice string, and candy corn

- icing to use as a "glue"

What to Do

1. Help your child examine the different candies. Talk about the properties of the candies.

2. Explain that you will be making candy creatures. Work together to choose candies that would make good arms, legs, bodies, faces, and so on.

3. Construct as many creatures as you can design. Examples might be spiders or other bugs, animals, and so on. Use the icing to "glue" the different parts together.

4. Share your creatures with the rest of your family.

Activity Materials from Home

Dear Family Member:

To do the activities in this chapter, we will need some materials that you may have around the house. Please note the items at the right. If possible, please send these things to school with your child.

Your help and support are appreciated!

____ **objects such as a rock, red marble, piece of yellow fabric**
____ **different-size plastic containers**
____ **balloon**
____ **plastic soft drink bottle**

Harcourt

La escuela y la casa

Harcourt Ciencias

Contenido del capítulo

Hoy comenzamos un nuevo capítulo de ciencias. Su hijo(a) aprenderá sobre la materia, los sólidos, los líquidos y los gases. Realizaremos actividades científicas que exploran las propiedades de los sólidos, los líquidos y los gases, qué hace que los objetos floten o se hundan y cómo podemos cambiar la materia.

Destrezas del proceso científico

Aprender a **recopilar y anotar datos** es una destreza importante de las ciencias. Para animar a su hijo(a) a practicar a recopilar y anotar datos, busque objetos en su casa que puedan flotar o hundirse. Hundir y flotar son propiedades físicas de una materia. Pida a su hijo que prediga si cada uno de los objetos se hundirá o flotará. Ayude a su hijo(a) a anotar sus predicciones. Luego pruebe los objetos y anote lo que observó. Ayude a su hijo(a) a comprender que anotar datos hace más fácil recordar lo que ha pasado y hablar de las observaciones con otros. Esto también ayuda a sacar conclusiones de lo que se ha observado.

Diversión

La materia tiene propiedades físicas diferentes.

Criaturas de dulce

Lo que necesitas

- caramelos surtidos, gomitas, trocitos de chocolate, dulce de malvavisco y dulce de regaliz
- glaseado para usar como "pegamento"

Lo que vas a hacer

1. Ayude a su hijo(a) a examinar los diferentes caramelos. Hable sobre las propiedades de los caramelos.

2. Explique que harán criaturas de dulce. Trabajen para elegir caramelos que formarán buenos brazos, piernas, cuerpos, caras y así sucesivamente.

3. Construyan tantas criaturas como las que puedan diseñar. Los ejemplos pueden ser arañas u otros insectos, animales y así sucesivamente. Usen el glaseado para "pegar" las diferentes partes.

4. Compartan sus criaturas con el resto de la familia.

Materiales de casa para la actividad

Querido familiar:

Para hacer las actividades en este capítulo, necesitaremos algunos materiales que tal vez tenga en la casa. Observe los artículos de la lista de la derecha. Si es posible, por favor envíe estas cosas con su hijo(a) a la escuela.

¡Gracias por su ayuda y su apoyo!

____ **objetos como una roca, una canica roja, un pedazo de tela amarilla**
____ **diferentes tamaños de recipientes de plástico**
____ **globo**
____ **botella de refresco de plástico**

Harcourt

School-Home Connection

Harcourt Science

Chapter Content

Our science class is beginning a chapter about sound. In this chapter your child will learn how vibrations make sounds, how we hear sounds, how sounds can vary in loudness and pitch, and how sounds are used to make music.

Science Process Skills

Investigating is one of the science process skills emphasized in this chapter. When scientists investigate a problem, they test different ideas. In this activity you and your child can investigate how our ears help us hear sounds.

Suggest to your child that two ears are better than one. Talk about why this might be true. Then test your ideas with a loudly ticking alarm clock, or an other object you can move and use to make sounds. Ask your child to close his or her eyes. Then hide the clock somewhere in the room. Have your child cover both ears and try to locate the clock by listening. Repeat with just one ear covered, then with both ears uncovered. Your child will probably discover that it's much easier to find the noisemaker with both ears. You might investigate further by trying to locate the sound by listening through a cardboard tube.

ScienceFun

Lesson 2 of this chapter focuses on how sounds are different. This activity will help your child become a more careful and discerning listener.

With your child, make up different categories of sounds to listen for, such as Outside Sounds, Inside Sounds, Street Sounds, Park Sounds, Animal Sounds, and Store Sounds. At home and as you visit different places, spend a few minutes listening carefully for sounds. Write down the sounds your child describes. Then talk about what makes each sound, and whether the sounds are loud or soft, high or low, pleasant or unpleasant. You may wish to work together to make a chart listing and describing the sounds you collect.

As you visit different places, your child can add new sounds and categories to the chart, such as School Sounds, Night Sounds, Morning Sounds, and Mealtime Sounds.

Activity Materials from Home

Dear Family Member:

To do the activities in this chapter, we will need some materials that you may have around the house. Please note the items listed at the right. If possible, please send these things to school with your child.

Your help and support are appreciated!

____ cardboard tube
____ foil
____ small coffee can
____ beans
____ balloon

Harcourt

La escuela y la casa

Contenido del capítulo

En nuestra clase de ciencias estamos comenzando un capítulo acerca del sonido. En este capítulo su niño(a) aprenderá cómo las vibraciones producen sonidos, cómo los sonidos pueden variar en volumen y tono y cómo los sonidos se usan para crear música.

Destrezas del proceso científico

Investigar es una de las destrezas del proceso de las ciencias que se enfatizan en este capítulo. Cuando los científicos investigan un problema, ponen a prueba diferentes ideas. En esta actividad Ud. y su niño(a) pueden investigar cómo nuestros oídos nos ayudan a escuchar los sonidos.

Comente con su niño(a) que tener dos oídos es mejor que tener uno. Comenten acerca de por qué esto pudiera ser verdadero. Luego pongan a prueba sus ideas usando un reloj despertador que produzca un fuerte tictac, u otro objeto que se pueda mover y usar para producir sonidos. Pida a su niño(a) que cierre sus ojos. Luego esconda el despertador en algún lugar de la habitación. Pida a su niño(a) que cubra sus oídos y que trate de encontrar el despertador guiándose por el sonido. Repita cubriendo solo un oído y luego descubriendo ambos oídos. Su niño(a) probablemente llegará a la conclusión de que es mucho más fácil encontrar el objeto que produce el sonido cuando usa ambos oídos. Pueden investigar más ampliamente al tratando de localizar el sonido, pero ahora escuchando a través de un tubo de cartón.

Diversión

La lección 2 de este capítulo está enfocada a aprender de qué manera los sonidos son diferentes. Esta actividad ayudará a su niño(a) a aprender a escuchar con más cuidado para tener una mejor comprensión.

Con su niño(a) forme diferentes categorías de sonidos que deseen buscar, tales como sonidos de afuera, sonidos de adentro, sonidos de la calle, sonidos del parque, sonidos de animales y sonidos de las tiendas. En casa, y mientras visita diferentes lugares, dedique algunos minutos para tratar de encontrar sonidos diferentes. Escriba acerca de los sonidos que su niño(a) describa. Luego, comenten acerca de qué es lo que produce a cada sonido y si los sonidos son agudos o graves, agradables o desagradables. Probablemente deseen trabajar juntos para hacer una tabla listando y describiendo los sonidos que coleccionen.

Mientras visiten diferentes lugares, su niño(a) puede agregar nuevos sonidos y categorías a la tabla, tales como sonidos de la escuela, sonidos de la noche, sonidos de la mañana y sonidos de la horas de las comidas.

Materiales de casa para la actividad

Querido familiar:

Para hacer las actividades de este capítulo, necesitaremos algunos materiales que tal vez tenga alrededor de la casa. Observe los artículos de la lista de la derecha. Si es posible, por favor envíe estas cosas con su hijo(a) a la escuela.

¡Gracias por su ayuda y apoyo!

_____ **tubos de cartón**
_____ **papel aluminio**
_____ **latas de café pequeñas**
_____ **frijoles**
_____ **globos**

TR22 • **Recursos de enseñanza**   **Unidad E - Capítulo 2**

School-Home Connection

Harcourt Science

Chapter Content

Today we begin a new chapter in science. Your child will be learning about what makes things move. We will be doing many activities, including investigating what will make something move, grouping objects that move the same way, and predicting how an object might change its motion.

Science Process Skills

Prediction is an important science skill. Scientific predictions are based on observations and inferences about those observations. You can help your child practice making predictions.

With your child, observe moving objects such as toys or vehicles in and around your home. After watching these objects, have your child predict things such as how far or fast something might travel or how long a toy might move. If you make the Come-Back Can described under *Science Fun,* try rolling the cans at different speeds and having your child predict what will happen.

Science Fun

Make a toy that seems to move by itself!

Come-Back Can

What You Need

- coffee can with ends removed (tape over sharp edges)
- 2 plastic lids that fit the can
- long rubber band • scissors
- fishing weight • 2 toothpicks

What to Do

1. Have an adult use scissors to punch a hole in each can lid (center).

2. Push one end of the rubber band through the hole from the inside and secure it over a toothpick. Thread the weight through the rubber band. Snap the lid on one end of the can. Attach the other end of the rubber band to the second lid and snap on the can.

3. Roll the can away from you. Observe what happens.

Activity Materials from Home

Dear Family Member:

To do the activities in this chapter, we will need some materials that you might have around the house. Please note the items at the right. If possible, please send these things to school with your child.

Your help and support are appreciated!

____ **plastic straws**
____ **craft sticks**
____ **rubber bands**
____ **string**
____ **plastic egg**
____ **toilet paper roll**

La escuela y la casa

Harcourt Ciencias

Contenido del capítulo

Hoy comenzamos un nuevo capítulo de ciencias. Su hijo(a) aprenderá qué hace que las cosas se muevan. Realizaremos actividades científicas para investigar qué hace que algo se mueva, agrupar objetos que se mueven en la misma dirección y predecir cómo un objeto podría cambiar su dirección.

Destrezas del proceso científico

Predecir es una destreza importante de las ciencias. Las predicciones científicas son basadas en observaciones e inferencias sobre esas observaciones. Ud. puede ayudar a su hijo(a) a practicar a hacer predicciones.

Con su hijo(a), observe objetos como juguetes o vehículos de su casa y su alrededor. Después de observar estos objetos, pida a su hijo(a) que prediga cosas como qué tan lejos o rápido puede ir algo o por cuánto tiempo se moverá un juguete. Si hace la Lata que se devuelve descrita en la sección de *Diversión*, trate de rodar los envases a velocidades diferentes y pida a su hijo(a) que prediga lo que pasará.

Diversión

¡Hacer un juguete que parece moverse por sí mismo!

La lata que se devuelve

Lo que necesitas

- una lata de café sin fondo (colocar cinta adhesiva a los bordes afilados)
- 2 tapas de plástico que le sirvan a la lata
- elástico grande
- tijeras
- plomos de pescar
- 2 palillos de dientes

Lo que vas a hacer

1. Pide a un adulto que use las tijeras para hacer un hueco en cada tapa del envase (en el centro).

2. Empuja una de las puntas del elástico por dentro a través del agujero de una de las tapas y asegúralo con un palillo de dientes. Inserta el plomo a través del elástico. Ata la otra punta del elástico a la otra tapa y sujétala a la tapa.

3. Rueda la lata lejos de ti. Observa qué sucede.

Materiales de casa para la actividad

Querido familiar:

Para hacer las actividades de este capítulo, necesitaremos algunos materiales que tal vez tenga en la casa. Observe los artículos de la lista de la derecha. Si es posible, por favor envíe estas cosas con su hijo(a) a la escuela.

¡Gracias por su ayuda y apoyo!

____ **pajitas plásticas**
____ **palitos**
____ **elásticos**
____ **hilo**
____ **huevo de plástico**
____ **rollo de papel de baño**

Harcourt

School-Home Connection

Harcourt Science

Chapter Content

Today we begin a new chapter in science. Your child will learn about magnets. We will be doing activities that help us understand what a magnet can do, where the poles of a magnet are located, and the types of things that can be magnetized.

Science Process Skills

Learning to **draw conclusions** is an important skill in science. Drawing conclusions is done after observations are made. Drawing conclusions based on observation is how we make sense of the world around us.

To give your child practice in making observations and drawing conclusions from those observations, observe and experiment with magnets around the house. Give your child an assortment of objects, such as paper clips, pencils, and various types of hardware. Make sure that some of the materials will be attracted to a magnet, and others won't. Have your child test the different objects, and observe what happens. Then help your child draw a conclusion about what types of things are attracted to magnets. (The objects that are attracted to a magnet contain the metal iron.)

Science Fun

Picture Magnets

What You Need

- strip of magnetic tape
- favorite photo
- glue
- cardboard
- cookie cutter
- scissors

What to Do

1. Trace the shape of the cookie cutter onto the cardboard and the photo, making sure to include the part of the photo you want on your finished magnet.
2. Cut out both shapes.
3. Glue the photo to the cardboard.
4. Glue the strip of magnetic tape to the back of the cardboard. Let dry.
5. Use your magnet to decorate the refrigerator or give to a friend!

Activity Materials from Home

Dear Family Member:

To do the activities in this chapter, we will need some materials that you may have around the house. Please note the items listed at the right. If possible, please send these things to school with your child.

Your help and support are appreciated!

____ **small objects such as buttons, barrettes, nails, marbles, balls, and jacks**
____ **piece of carpet**
____ **cardboard box**

Harcourt

La escuela y la casa

Harcourt Ciencias

Contenido del capítulo

Hoy comenzamos un nuevo capítulo de ciencias. Su hijo(a) aprenderá sobre los imanes. Realizaremos actividades científicas que ayudarán a comprender qué puede hacer un imán, dónde se encuentran ubicados los polos de los imanes y los tipos de cosas que se pueden magnetizar.

Destrezas del proceso científico

Aprender a **sacar conclusiones** es una destreza importante de las ciencias. Sacar conclusiones se hace después de que se han hecho las observaciones. Sacar conclusiones basadas en una observación es como le damos sentido al mundo que nos rodea.

Para hacer que su hijo(a) practique observar y sacar conclusiones de estas observaciones, observe y experimente con imanes en su casa. Dele a su hijo(a) una serie de objetos como clips, lápices y varios tipos de objetos metálicos. Asegúrese de que algunos de estos materiales serán atraídos por el imán y otros no. Pida a su hijo(a) que pruebe los diferentes objetos y observe qué sucede. Luego ayude a su hijo(a) a sacar una conclusión sobre qué tipo de cosas son atraídas por los imanes. (Los objetos que son atraídos por un imán contienen el metal hierro.)

Diversión

Imanes de fotografías

Lo que necesitas

- tira de cinta adhesiva magnética
- fotografía favorita
- pegamento
- cartulina
- cortador de galletas
- tijeras

Lo que vas a hacer

1. Traza la figura del cortador de galletas en la cartulina y en la fotografía asegurándote de incluir la parte de la fotografía que quieres cuando termines tu imán.

2. Corta ambas figuras.

3. Pega la fotografía en la cartulina.

4. Pega la tira de cinta adhesiva magnética en la parte trasera de la cartulina. Déjala secar.

5. Usa tu imán para decorar el refrigerador o dárselo a un amigo.

Materiales de casa para la actividad

Querido familiar:

Para hacer las actividades en este capítulo, necesitaremos algunos materiales que tal vez tenga en la casa. Observe los artículos de la lista de la derecha. Si es posible, por favor envíe estas cosas con su hijo(a) a la escuela.

¡Gracias por su ayuda y su apoyo!

____ **objetos pequeños como botones, hebillas, clavos, canicas, pelotas y matatenas**
____ **pedazos de alfombra**
____ **caja de cartulina**

Name _____   Date _____

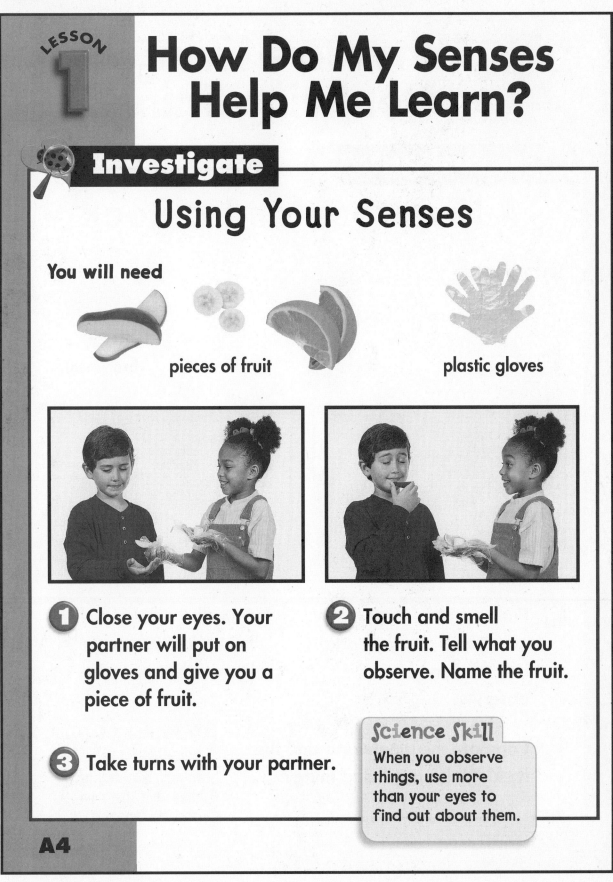

Name _____ Date _____

What Are Living and Nonliving Things?

Investigate

A Mealworm and a Rock

You will need

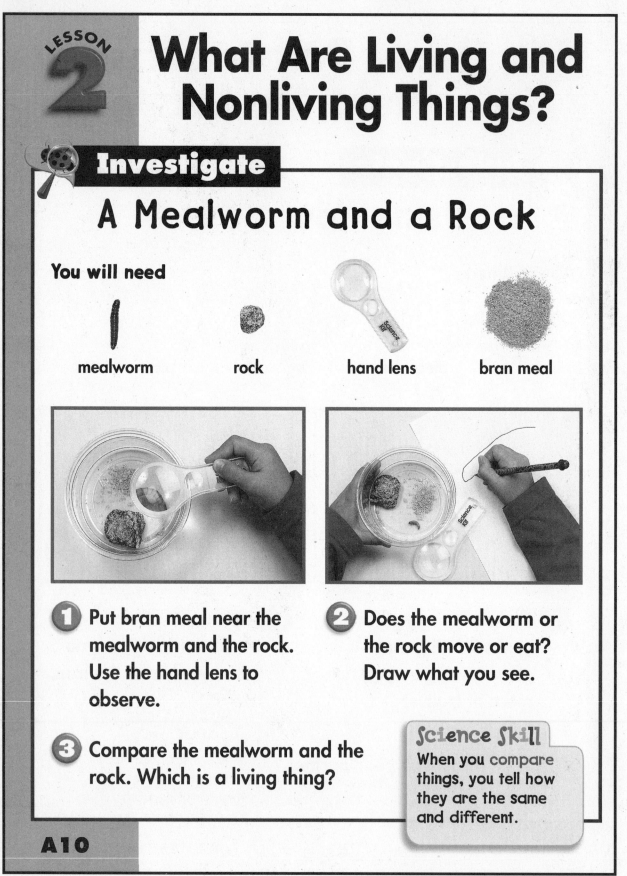

mealworm   rock   hand lens   bran meal

1 Put bran meal near the mealworm and the rock. Use the hand lens to observe.

2 Does the mealworm or the rock move or eat? Draw what you see.

3 Compare the mealworm and the rock. Which is a living thing?

Science Skill
When you compare things, you tell how they are the same and different.

A10

Harcourt

LESSON 1

What Are the Parts of a Plant?

Investigate

Plant Parts

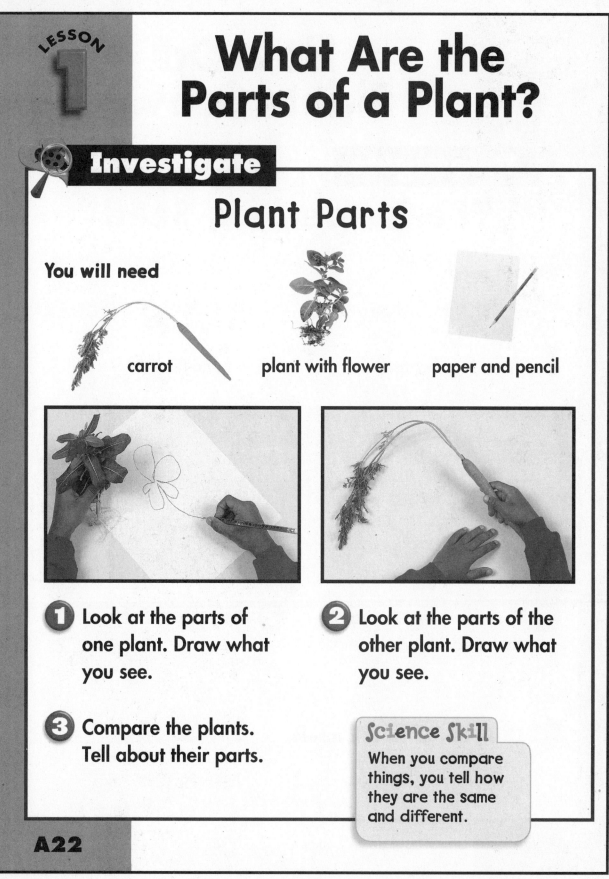

You will need

carrot   plant with flower   paper and pencil

1 Look at the parts of one plant. Draw what you see.

2 Look at the parts of the other plant. Draw what you see.

3 Compare the plants. Tell about their parts.

Science Skill
When you compare things, you tell how they are the same and different.

A22

Harcourt

LESSON 2

How Do Plants Grow?

Investigate

The Inside of a Seed

You will need

bean seed

hand lens

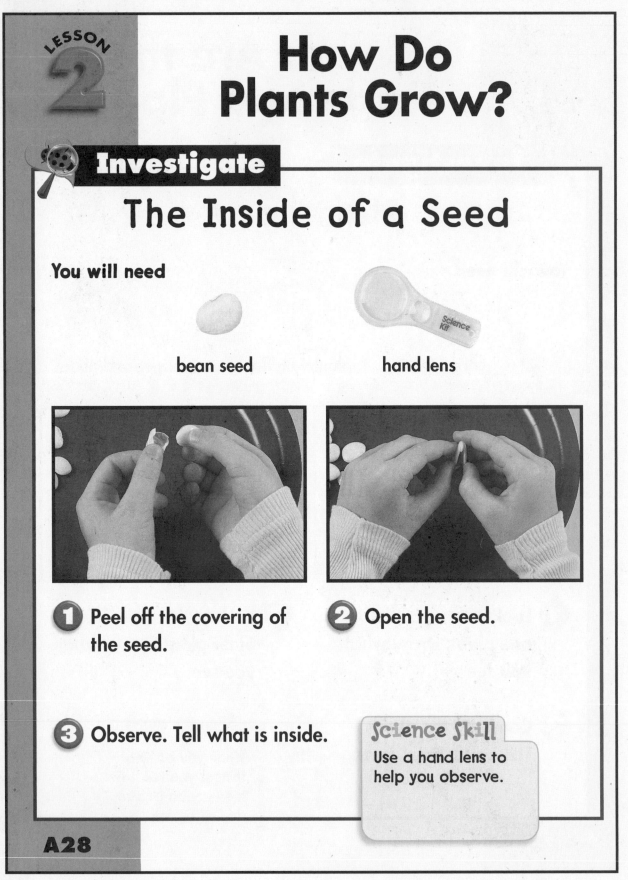

1 Peel off the covering of the seed.

2 Open the seed.

3 Observe. Tell what is inside.

Science Skill
Use a hand lens to help you observe.

A28

Harcourt

LESSON **3**

What Do Plants Need?

Investigate

What Plants Need to Grow

You will need

seeds   2 clear cups   any color cup   soil

1 Fill one clear cup with soil. Plant two seeds near the side. Water.

2 Put the cup with the seeds into the cup with color. After 3 days, take it out.

Science Skill
When you share your ideas, you communicate with others.

3 Share what you see.

Harcourt

A32

Name _____ Date _____

What Do Animals Need?

Investigate

An Animal Home

You will need

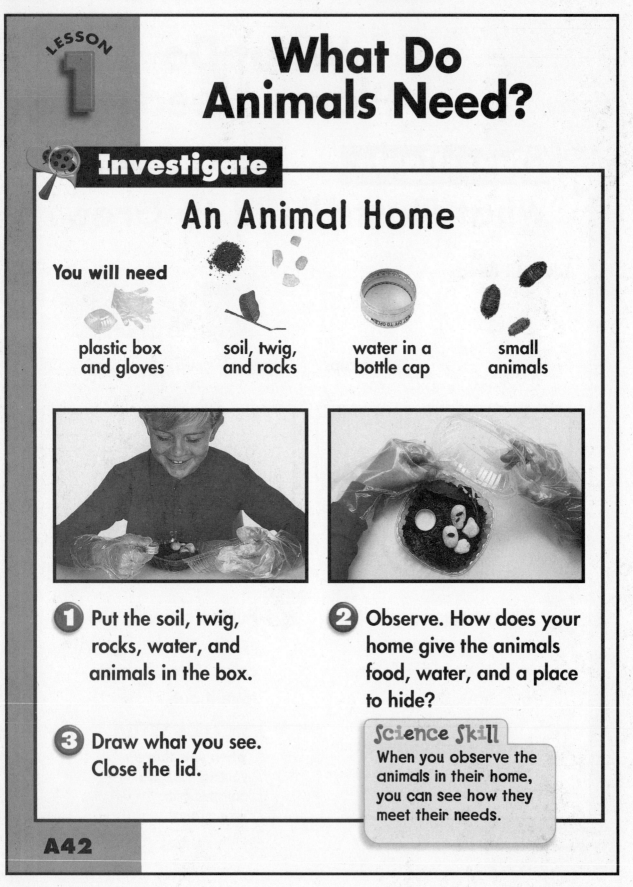

plastic box and gloves

soil, twig, and rocks

water in a bottle cap

small animals

1️⃣ Put the soil, twig, rocks, water, and animals in the box.

2️⃣ Observe. How does your home give the animals food, water, and a place to hide?

3️⃣ Draw what you see. Close the lid.

Science Skill
When you observe the animals in their home, you can see how they meet their needs.

A42

Harcourt

Use with page A42.

Name _____ Date _____

LESSON 2

What Are Some Kinds of Animals?

Investigate

Animals in Your Neighborhood

You will need

paper and pencil

1 Observe different kinds of animals in your schoolyard.

2 Draw a picture of each animal you observe.

3 Classify the animals into groups. How are the animals in each group the same?

Science Skill
When you classify animals, you observe how they are the same. Then you group them.

A48

Name _____ Date _____

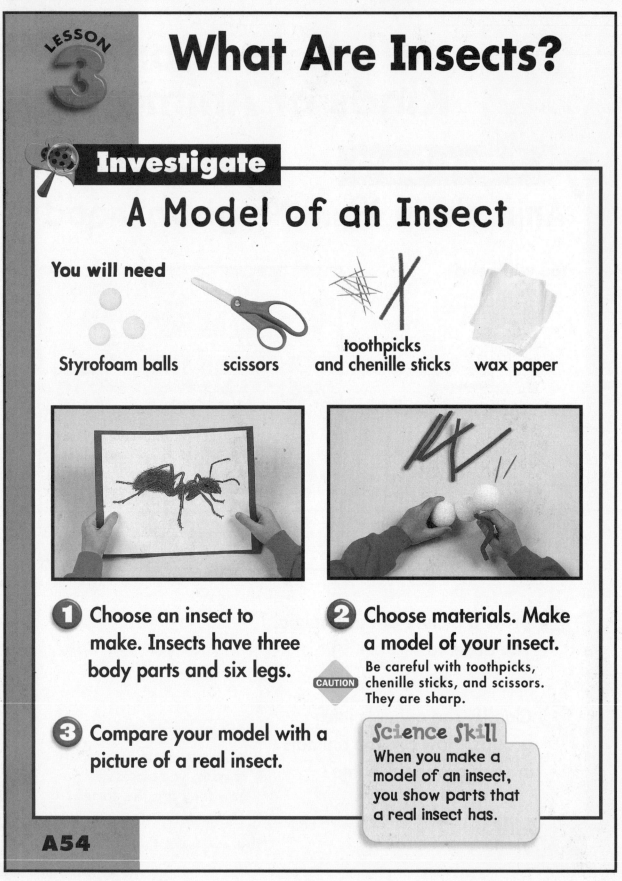

LESSON 3

What Are Insects?

Investigate

A Model of an Insect

You will need

Styrofoam balls   scissors   toothpicks and chenille sticks   wax paper

1 Choose an insect to make. Insects have three body parts and six legs.

2 Choose materials. Make a model of your insect.

CAUTION Be careful with toothpicks, chenille sticks, and scissors. They are sharp.

3 Compare your model with a picture of a real insect.

Science Skill
When you make a model of an insect, you show parts that a real insect has.

A54

Harcourt

LESSON **4**

How Do Animals Grow?

Investigate

Animals and Their Young

You will need

animal picture cards

paper and pencil

Animals and Their Young		
Animal	Same	Different
cats	Both have ears. Both are orange.	One is big. One is small.

1 Match the picture cards. Put each young animal with the adult.

2 Make a chart. Compare the young animal and the adult.

3 Tell how each young animal is like the adult. Tell how it is different.

Science Skill
When you compare the pictures, you tell how they are the same and different.

A58

Harcourt

LESSON **5**

How Does a Butterfly Grow?

Investigate

A Butterfly's Life

You will need

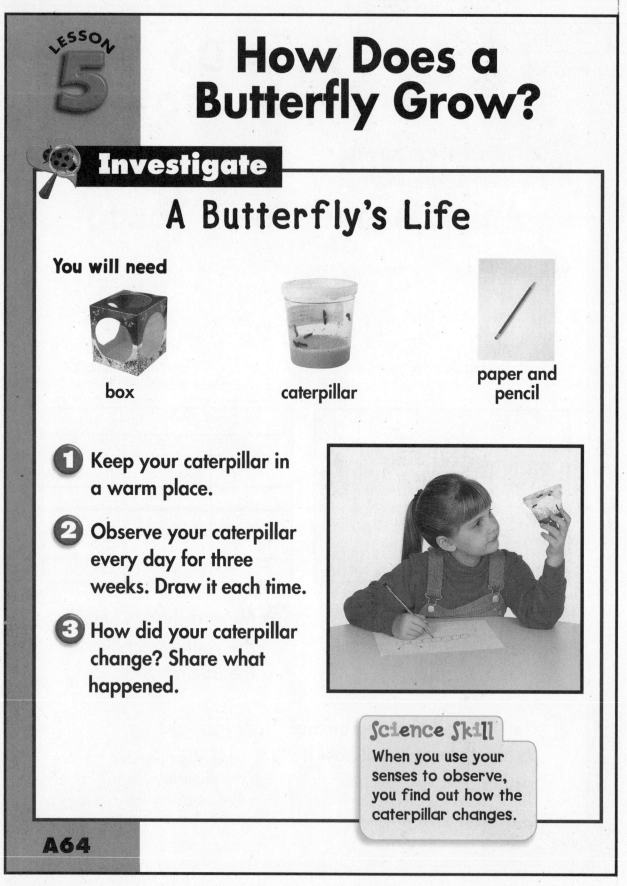

box

caterpillar

paper and pencil

1 Keep your caterpillar in a warm place.

2 Observe your caterpillar every day for three weeks. Draw it each time.

3 How did your caterpillar change? Share what happened.

Science Skill

When you use your senses to observe, you find out how the caterpillar changes.

A64

Harcourt

LESSON 6

How Does a Frog Grow?

Investigate

A Frog's Life

You will need

picture cards

1 Put the picture cards in sequence. Show how you think a frog changes as it grows.

2 Tell why you put your cards in the order you did.

Science Skill

When you sequence the cards, you show what happens first, next, and last.

A70

Harcourt

Name _____ Date _____

How Do Animals Need Plants?

LESSON 1

Investigate

How Small Animals Use Plants

You will need

timer or watch   string loop   paper and pencil

1 Go outside with your class. Observe animals and plants inside your string loop.

2 Observe and record for five minutes. How are animals using plants?

3 Share what you observed.

Science Skill
As you observe, use your senses of sight, hearing, and smell to help you.

B4

Harcourt

Name _____   Date _____

How Do Animals Help Plants?

Investigate

How Seeds Stick to Animals

You will need

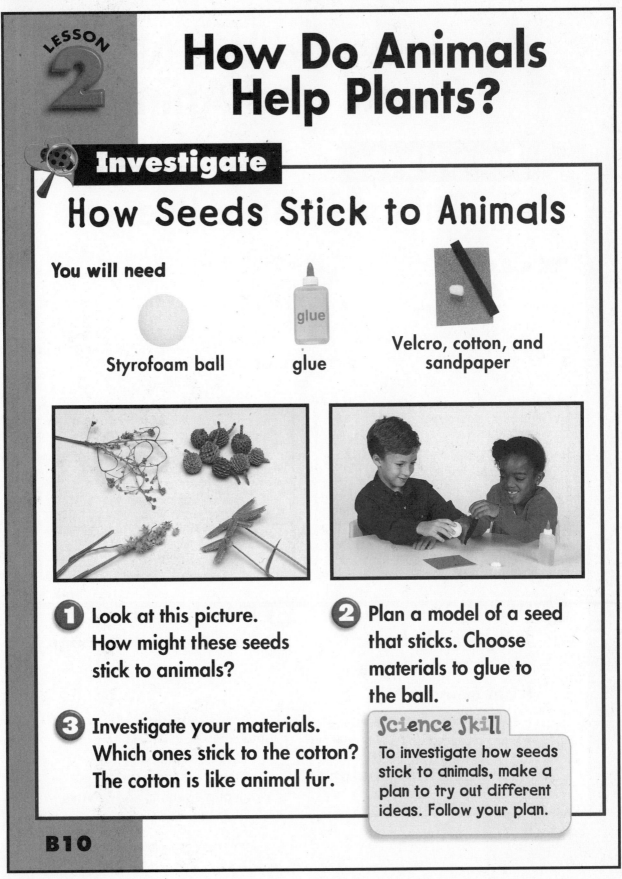

Styrofoam ball   glue   Velcro, cotton, and sandpaper

1 Look at this picture. How might these seeds stick to animals?

2 Plan a model of a seed that sticks. Choose materials to glue to the ball.

3 Investigate your materials. Which ones stick to the cotton? The cotton is like animal fur.

Science Skill
To investigate how seeds stick to animals, make a plan to try out different ideas. Follow your plan.

B10

LESSON 3

How Do We Need Plants and Animals?

Investigate

Things People Use

You will need

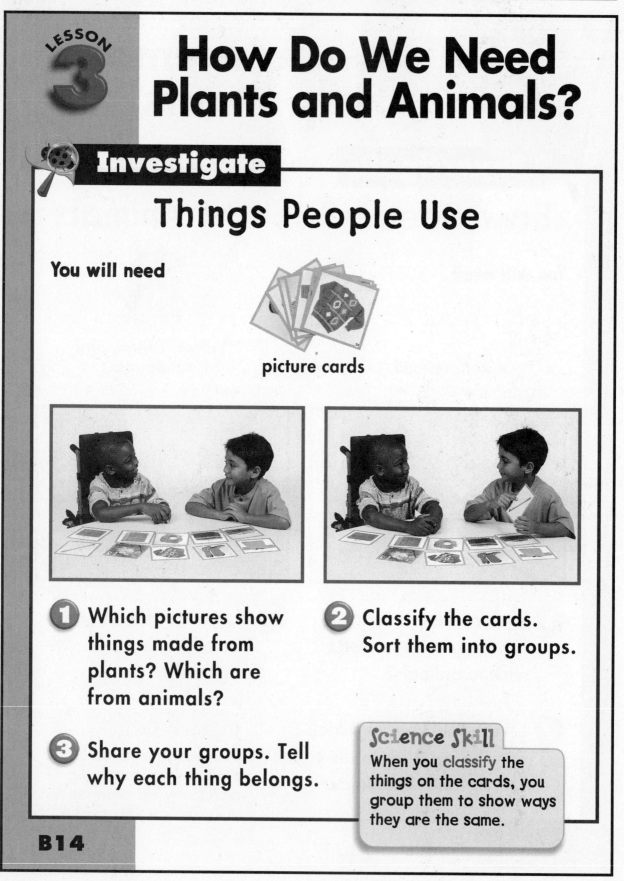

picture cards

1 Which pictures show things made from plants? Which are from animals?

2 Classify the cards. Sort them into groups.

3 Share your groups. Tell why each thing belongs.

Science Skill
When you classify the things on the cards, you group them to show ways they are the same.

B14

Harcourt

What Lives in a Forest?

LESSON 1

Investigate

Forest Trees

You will need

dark crayon

pencil and paper

1 Go outside. Find a tree. Draw one of its leaves.

2 Make a rubbing of the tree's bark.

3 Compare your drawing and rubbing with a classmate's.

Science Skill
When you compare drawings and rubbings, look for ways the trees are the same and different.

B26

LESSON 2

What Lives in the Desert?

Investigate

Desert Leaves

You will need

2 paper clips   water   wax paper   2 paper-towel leaf shapes

1. Make both leaf shapes damp. Put one shape on wax paper. Fold the paper over. Clip it.

2. Put both leaves in the sunlight. Check them after an hour.

3. Which leaf holds water longer? Draw a conclusion.

Science Skill
To draw a conclusion about desert leaves, think about your leaf with the waxy coat and the other leaf.

Harcourt

B30

LESSON 3

What Lives in a Rain Forest?

Investigate

Rain Forest Plants

You will need

seeds

2 wet cotton balls

film cans and lid with hole

plastic and rubber band

wet cotton ball

seeds

wet cotton ball

seeds

plastic

rubber band

1 Some rain forest plants get little light. Make a model of a rain forest like this one. Close lid.

3 Set both models in the sun for 5 days. Tell how the cotton changes.

2 Plants in open areas get more light. Make a model of an open area.

Science Skill
To communicate how the forests grew, draw and share pictures of what you observed.

B34

Harcourt

Name _____ Date _____

LESSON 4

What Lives in the Ocean?

Investigate

Ocean Animals

You will need

ocean picture cards

1 Which ocean pictures show fish? Which show other animals?

2 Classify the animals. Put them in groups.

3 Share your groups. Talk about other ways to classify the animals.

Science Skill
When you classify the animals, you group them to show ways they are the same.

B38

Harcourt

Name _____ Date _____

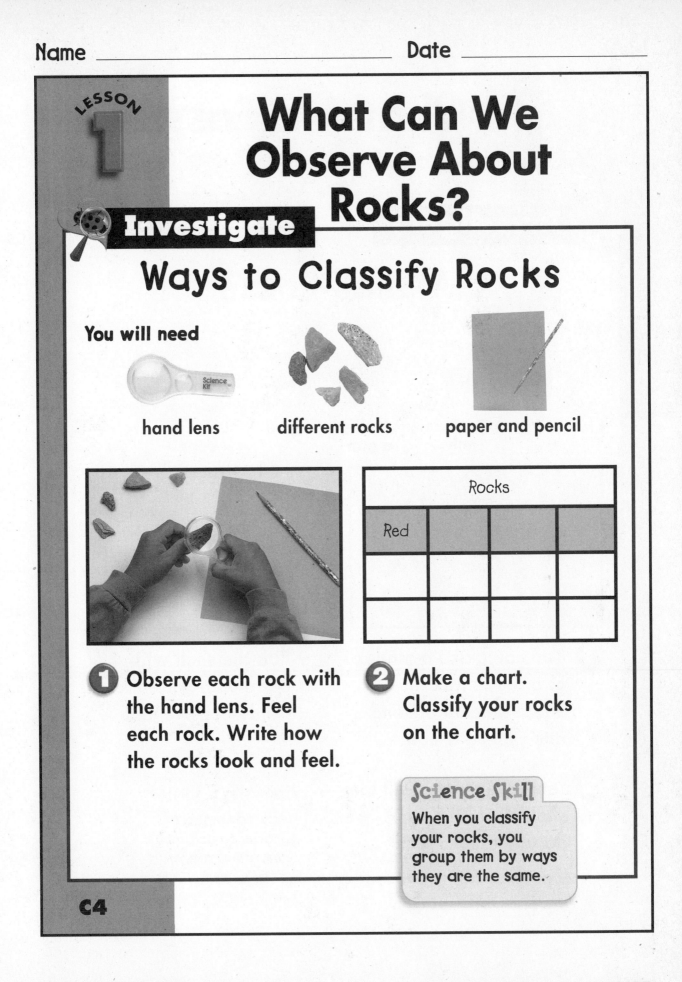

What Can We Observe About Rocks?

Investigate

Ways to Classify Rocks

You will need

hand lens   different rocks   paper and pencil

Rocks			
Red			

1 Observe each rock with the hand lens. Feel each rock. Write how the rocks look and feel.

2 Make a chart. Classify your rocks on the chart.

Science Skill

When you classify your rocks, you group them by ways they are the same.

C4

Harcourt

LESSON 2

What Are Fossils?

Investigate

A Shell Fossil

You will need

a shell   petroleum   sand in   glue   measuring   craft stick
         jelly   a pan   cup

1 You can make a model of a fossil. Mix an equal amount of sand and glue in a pan.

2 Rub the shell with petroleum jelly. Press it firmly into the mix.

3 Let the glue dry. Pull the shell out of the sand. What do you see?

Science Skill

You can make a model to help you understand how fossils form.

C8

Harcourt

LESSON **3**

What Have We Learned from Fossils?

Investigate

Animals Then and Now

You will need

picture cards

1 You can compare animal fossils with animals of today. You and a partner each take one of the sets of cards.

2 Your partner will put down a card that shows an animal fossil or an animal of today. Put down the matching card.

3 Take turns. Play until all the animal cards are matched.

Science Skill
When you compare animals of long ago and today, look for ways they are the same.

C12

Harcourt

LESSON
1

What Are Natural Resources?

Investigate

The World Around You

You will need

paper and pencil

Things I Saw Outdoors	
animals	
plants	
water	
land	
soil	

1 Make a chart like this one. Then go outdoors. Gather data about what you observe.

2 Look for the things on your chart. Make a tally mark to record what you see.

3 Compare with a classmate. Did you see the same things or different things?

Science Skill
To gather data, observe and record what you see.

C22

Harcourt

LESSON 2

Where Is Air on Earth?

Investigate

Air in a Bag

You will need

plastic bag

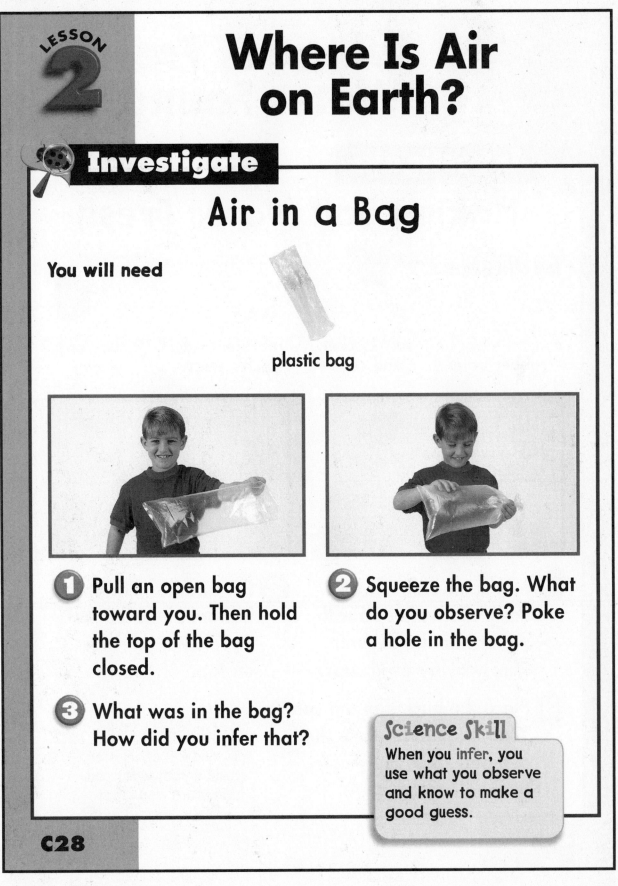

① Pull an open bag toward you. Then hold the top of the bag closed.

② Squeeze the bag. What do you observe? Poke a hole in the bag.

③ What was in the bag? How did you infer that?

Science Skill
When you infer, you use what you observe and know to make a good guess.

C28

Harcourt

LESSON 3

Where Is Fresh Water Found?

Investigate

Making Salt Water Fresh

You will need

rubber band

salt, bucket, and sand

marbles and plastic wrap

2 cups and water

1 Mix some salt in water. Taste the water. Pour the water into the bucket. Throw away used cups.

2 Put another cup in the bottom of the bucket. Cover. Put marbles on top.

3 Place the bucket in the sun. Wait two hours. Take the cup out. Taste the water. Draw a conclusion.

Science Skill

To draw a conclusion, think about what you observed and what you know about water.

C32

Harcourt

Use with page C32.

LESSON 4

How Can People Take Care of Resources?

Investigate

Reusing a Resource

You will need

one sheet of newspaper   tape   pencils

1 Fold the newspaper into a long strip.

2 Wind the strip tightly. Tape the top and the bottom.

3 Put pencils into the holder. Communicate how you made something new with the newspaper.

Science Skill
When you communicate, you share your ideas with others.

C36

Harcourt

Name _____ Date _____

LESSON 1

What Is Weather?

Investigate

Weather Conditions

You will need

paper

markers

Daily Weather

Monday	Tuesday	Wednesday	Thursday	Friday

1 Observe the changes in weather for two weeks.

2 Make a chart. Draw or write what you observe on your chart.

3 Compare the daily weather changes you observed.

Science Skill

When you compare the things you observed, tell how they are the same and different.

D4

Harcourt

LESSON 2

What Is Temperature?

Investigate

Measuring Air Temperature

You will need

thermometer   paper and pencil   red crayon

1. Draw and label two thermometers.

2. Measure and record the air temperature in the classroom.

3. Put the thermometer outside for 5 minutes. Measure and record the air temperature.

4. Compare the temperatures.

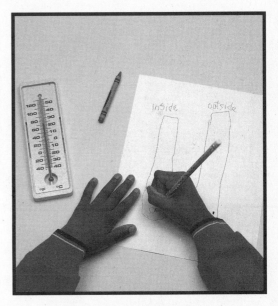

Science Skill
To measure temperature with a thermometer, read the number next to the top of the red line.

D8

Name _____ Date _____

LESSON 3

Investigate

What Is Wind?

Wind Direction

You will need

drinking straw   round toothpick   paper triangle   tape

1. Make a wind vane. Poke the toothpick through the straw.

   ⚠ **CAUTION** Be careful. Toothpicks are sharp.

2. Tape the triangle to the straw. Go outdoors. Hold up the toothpick.

3. Observe the wind's direction on two windy days.

Science Skill
To observe the wind's direction, check which way the triangle points.

D12

Harcourt

LESSON 4

What Makes Clouds and Rain?

Investigate

How Clouds Form

You will need

jar with lid   very warm water   ice cubes

1 Pour warm water into the jar. Wait. Pour out most of the water.

CAUTION Be careful. Water is hot!

2 Set the lid upside down on the jar. Observe the jar.

3 Put ice on the lid. Observe. Infer how clouds form.

Science Skill
To infer, first observe. Then think about what happened and draw a conclusion.

D16

Harcourt

LESSON 1

What Can We See in the Sky?

Investigate

The Sky

You will need

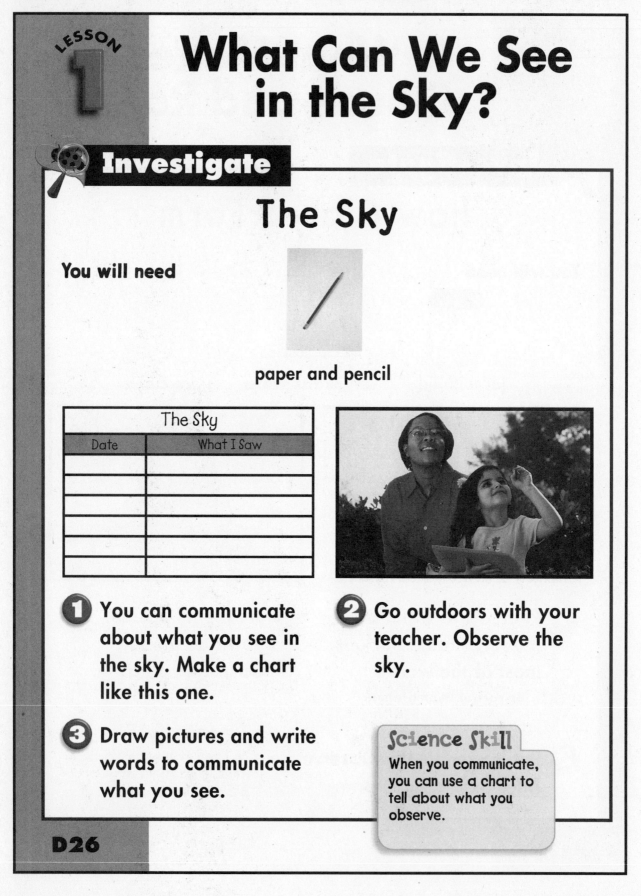

paper and pencil

The Sky	
Date	What I Saw

1 You can communicate about what you see in the sky. Make a chart like this one.

2 Go outdoors with your teacher. Observe the sky.

3 Draw pictures and write words to communicate what you see.

Science Skill
When you communicate, you can use a chart to tell about what you observe.

D26

Harcourt

Name _____   Date _____

Why Do We Have Day and Night?

Investigate

Day and Night

You will need

globe   flashlight   labels   tape

1. Make a model of the sun and Earth. The flashlight is the sun. The globe is Earth. Tape on the labels.

2. Ask a partner to hold Earth. Shine the flashlight on Earth. The side facing the sun is having day. The other side is having night.

3. Tell how the model helps you see why we have day and night.

Science Skill

When you make a model, you can use it to find out why something happens.

D30

Harcourt

What Is Spring?

LESSON 3

Investigate

What Helps Seeds Sprout

You will need

4 bean seeds   2 cups   mist bottle   paper towels   hand lens

1 Put a damp paper towel in each cup. Add two seeds to each. Label the cups *winter* and *spring*.

2 Put the *winter* cup in a cold, dark place. Put the *spring* cup in a warm, dark place.

3 Observe the seeds with the hand lens three days later. What can you infer?

Science Skill
To infer, first observe, and then think about what you see.

D34

Harcourt

LESSON 4

What Is Summer?

Investigate

Colors That Can Keep You Cool

You will need

4 thermometers   4 colors of paper   stapler   clock

1 Fold and staple 4 color sheets of paper to make sleeves. Put a thermometer in each. Place in the sun.

2 Record the starting temperatures for each.

3 Wait 30 minutes. Record the temperatures again. Order from hottest to coolest.

Science Skill

To put the colors in order, start with the one with the hottest temperature. End with the coolest.

D38

LESSON **5**

What Is Fall?

Investigate

Storing Apples

You will need

apple rings   string   plastic bag   paper and pencil

1 Put some apple rings in the plastic bag. Store them on a shelf.

2 Hang the other apple rings on string. Don't let them touch.

3 Predict and record what will happen.

4 Wait one week. Record.

Science Skill

To predict which way to store apple rings is better, use what you know about food. Then decide.

D42

Harcourt

LESSON 6

What Is Winter?

Investigate

Keeping Warm in Cold Weather

You will need

plastic bag

container of
ice water

things to keep
your hand warm

1 Put your hand in the bag. Then put your hand in the ice water. Does the bag keep your hand warm?

2 What could you put in the bag to keep your hand warm? Choose some things to try.

3 Investigate your ideas by trying them. Which one works best?

Science Skill
To investigate how to keep your hand warm, try out each of your ideas.

D46

Harcourt

LESSON 1

What Can We Observe About Solids?

Investigate

Solid Objects

You will need

objects

paper and pencil

1 Observe each object.

2 Compare the sizes, shapes, and colors of the objects.

3 Think of three ways to classify the objects. Draw or write them on your paper.

Science Skill
To classify the objects, find ways they are the same and group them.

E4

Harcourt

Name _____ Date _____

What Can We Observe About Liquids?

Investigate

Liquids in Bottles

You will need

3 containers   measuring cup   paper and pencil

1 Draw the shape of the water in each container.

2 Which container do you think has the most water?

3 Measure the water. Write a number for each container. Use the numbers to tell what you found out.

Science Skill
You can write numbers when you measure. Use the numbers to compare the things you measured.

E8

LESSON 3

What Objects Sink or Float?

Investigate

Shapes That Sink or Float

You will need

ball of clay   aquarium with water   paper and pencil

1 Gather data about shapes that sink or float. Put the clay ball in the water.

2 Record data about what happens.

3 Make the clay into different shapes. Do they sink or float? Record.

Science Skill

When you gather data, you observe things. When you record data, you write and draw what you observe.

E12

Harcourt

Name _____ Date _____

Harcourt

LESSON 4

What Solids Dissolve in Liquids?

Investigate

Solids in Water

You will need

stirring stick   paper and pencil   solids to test   4 cups of water

1 What do you think these solids will do in water? Form a hypothesis for each one.

2 Put a solid into water. Stir for a minute. When the water stops swirling, observe.

3 Can you see the solid in the water? Record what you observe. Repeat for the other solids.

Solids in Water				
	My hypothesis		My results	
	Will dissolve	Will not dissolve	Did dissolve	Did not dissolve
salt				
sand				
rocks				
baking soda				

Science Skill
When you form a hypothesis you choose and test a possible answer.

E16

Use with page E16.

Teaching Resources • TR65

Name _____ Date _____

What Can We Observe About Gases?

Investigate

Air in a Bottle

You will need

balloon

plastic soft drink bottle

1 Squeeze the bottle to observe the air in it. Blow up the balloon. Feel the air come out.

2 Put the balloon in the bottle. Pull the end over the top.

3 Try to blow up the balloon. What else is in the bottle? Draw a conclusion.

Science Skill
To draw a conclusion about what happened, think about what you observed.

E20

Harcourt

LESSON 6

How Can We Change Objects?

Investigate

Changing Paper

You will need

4 cards with slits   paints and brushes   glitter   glue   paper and pencil

1 Observe the cards. Record how they look and feel.

2 How could you change the way the cards look and feel? Investigate your ideas.

3 Record how you change the cards.

Science Skill
To investigate, think of changes you could make, and then try them out.

E24

Name _____   Date _____

What Are Sounds?

Investigate

Sounds

You will need

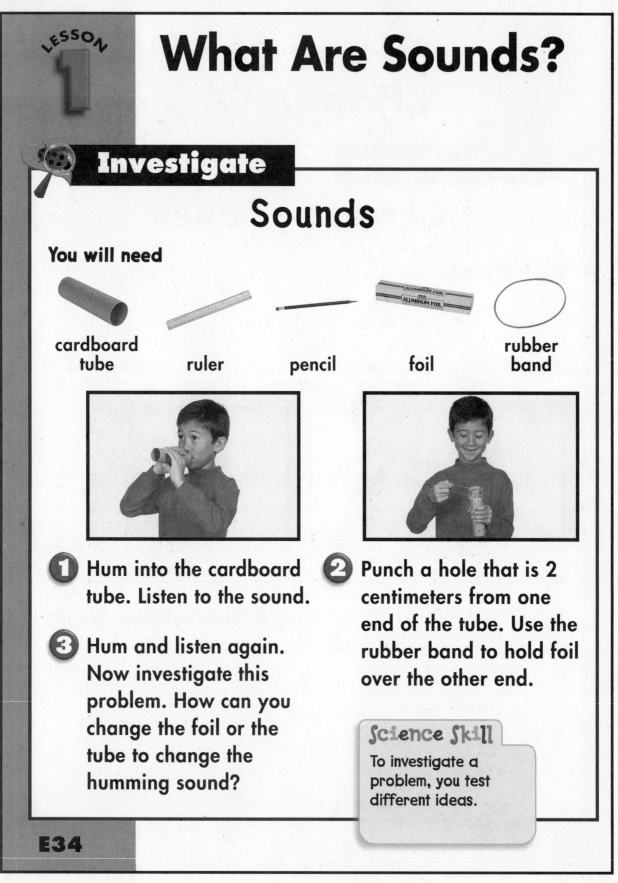

cardboard tube   ruler   pencil   foil   rubber band

1 Hum into the cardboard tube. Listen to the sound.

2 Punch a hole that is 2 centimeters from one end of the tube. Use the rubber band to hold foil over the other end.

3 Hum and listen again. Now investigate this problem. How can you change the foil or the tube to change the humming sound?

Science Skill

To investigate a problem, you test different ideas.

E34

Harcourt

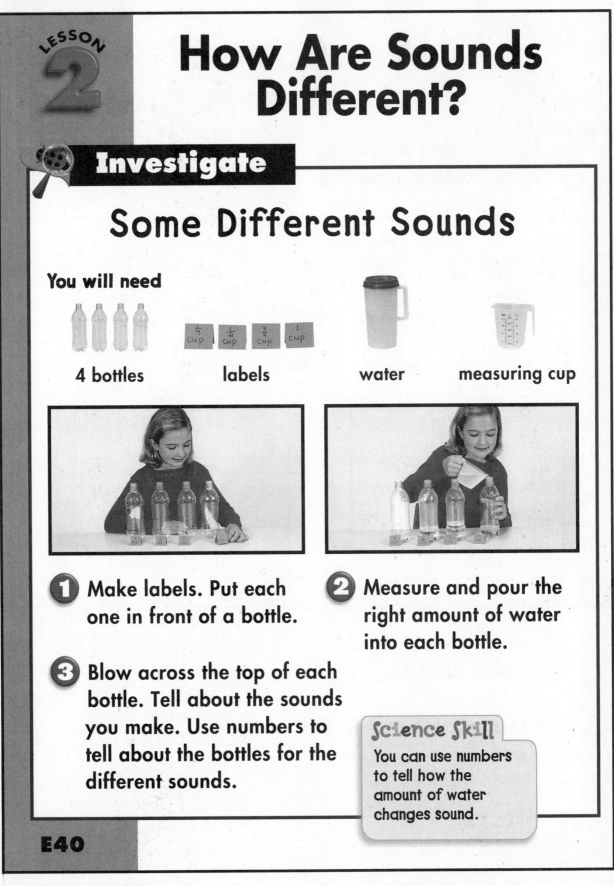

LESSON 2

How Are Sounds Different?

Investigate

Some Different Sounds

You will need

4 bottles   labels   water   measuring cup

1. Make labels. Put each one in front of a bottle.

2. Measure and pour the right amount of water into each bottle.

3. Blow across the top of each bottle. Tell about the sounds you make. Use numbers to tell about the bottles for the different sounds.

Science Skill
You can use numbers to tell how the amount of water changes sound.

E40

Harcourt

What Sounds Do Instruments Make?

LESSON 3

Investigate

Making Your Own Drum

You will need

a small can   beans   balloon   rubber band   pencil with eraser

1 Put the beans into the can. Stretch the balloon over the top. Put the rubber band on.

2 Form a hypothesis about your drum. What kind of sound will it make? What will vibrate?

3 Test your hypothesis. Use the pencil to beat the drum. Listen for the sounds.

Science Skill
When you form a hypothesis, you choose and test a possible answer.

E46

Harcourt

       Use with page E46.

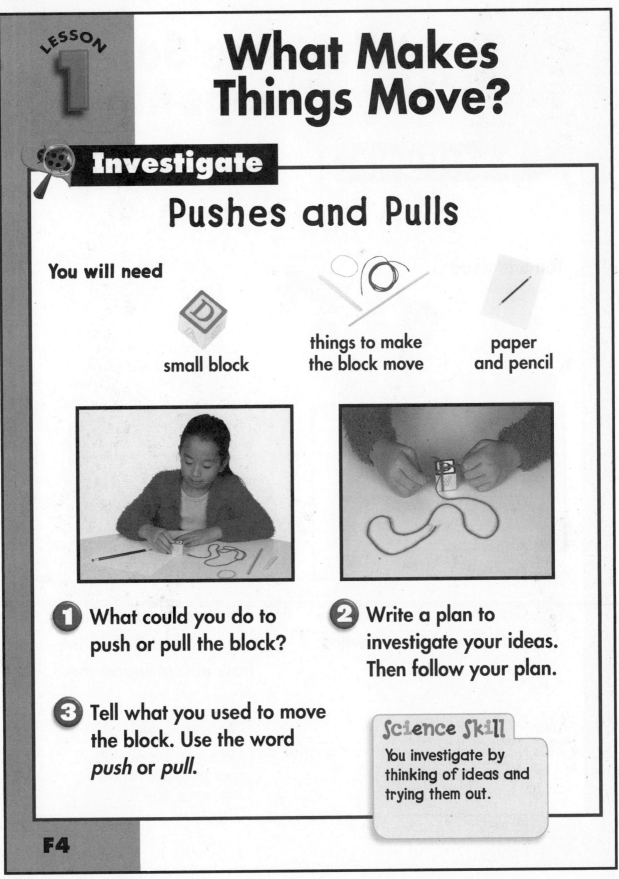

What Makes Things Move?

Investigate

Pushes and Pulls

You will need

small block

things to make
the block move

paper
and pencil

1 What could you do to push or pull the block?

2 Write a plan to investigate your ideas. Then follow your plan.

3 Tell what you used to move the block. Use the word *push* or *pull.*

Science Skill
You investigate by thinking of ideas and trying them out.

F4

LESSON 2

What Are Some Ways Things Move?

Investigate

Moving Objects

You will need

objects   paper and pencil

1 Observe and record how each object moves when you push or pull it.

2 Group objects that move the same way. Write how you grouped them.

Science Skill

To group the objects, put those that move in the same way together.

F8

Harcourt

Why Do Things Move the Way They Do?

LESSON 3

Investigate

Predicting Motion

You will need

ramp   plastic ball    tape    block

1. Set up the ramp. Predict where the ball will stop. Mark that place with tape.

2. Let the ball roll down the ramp. Was your prediction right?

3. Now put the block where the ball will hit it. Do Step 2 again.

Science Skill

To predict where the ball will stop, think about how a ball rolls and bounces.

F12

Harcourt

Name _____   Date _____

LESSON 4

How Do Objects Move on Surfaces?

Investigate

Smooth and Rough Surfaces

You will need

ramp   toy truck   meterstick   paper and pencil

1. Set up a ramp on a smooth surface. Let the truck roll down.

2. Measure how far it rolls. Record the number. Do the same on a rough surface.

3. On which surface does the truck roll farther? Use your numbers to tell.

Science Skill

Measure how far the truck rolls from the end of the ramp to where the truck stops.

F18

Harcourt

LESSON 5

How Do Wheels Help Objects Move?

Investigate

Rollers

You will need

rollers   heavy book   toy truck   tape

1 Push the book. Then put rollers under it. Push again. Which is easier?

2 Push the truck. Tape the wheels, and push it again. Which is easier?

3 Draw a conclusion about wheels and rollers.

Science Skill
To draw a conclusion about something, use what you have observed to explain what happens.

F22

Harcourt

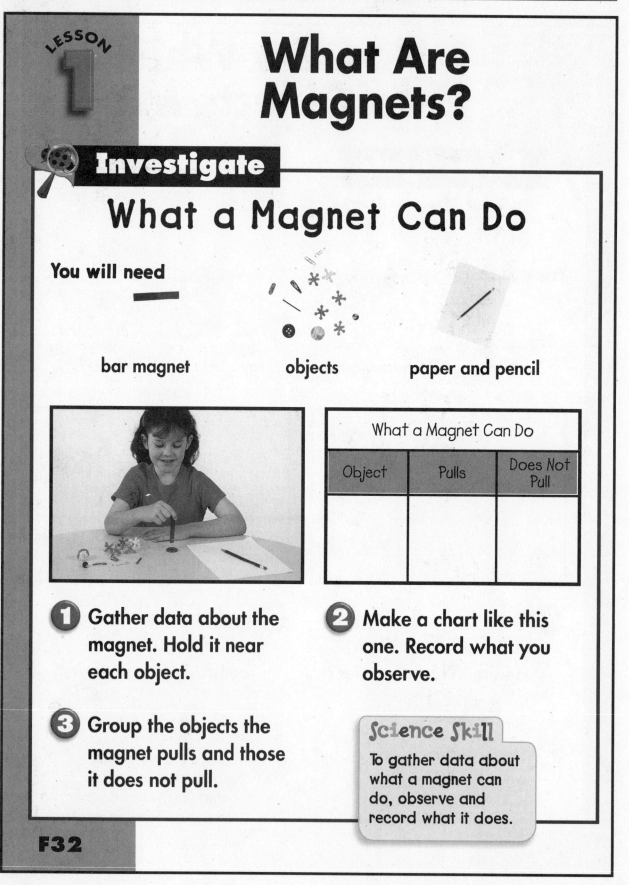

LESSON 1

What Are Magnets?

Investigate

What a Magnet Can Do

You will need

bar magnet   objects   paper and pencil

What a Magnet Can Do		
Object	Pulls	Does Not Pull

1 Gather data about the magnet. Hold it near each object.

2 Make a chart like this one. Record what you observe.

3 Group the objects the magnet pulls and those it does not pull.

Science Skill

To gather data about what a magnet can do, observe and record what it does.

F32

Harcourt

Name _____ Date _____

Harcourt

LESSON 2

What Are the Poles of a Magnet?

Investigate

A Magnet's Ends

You will need

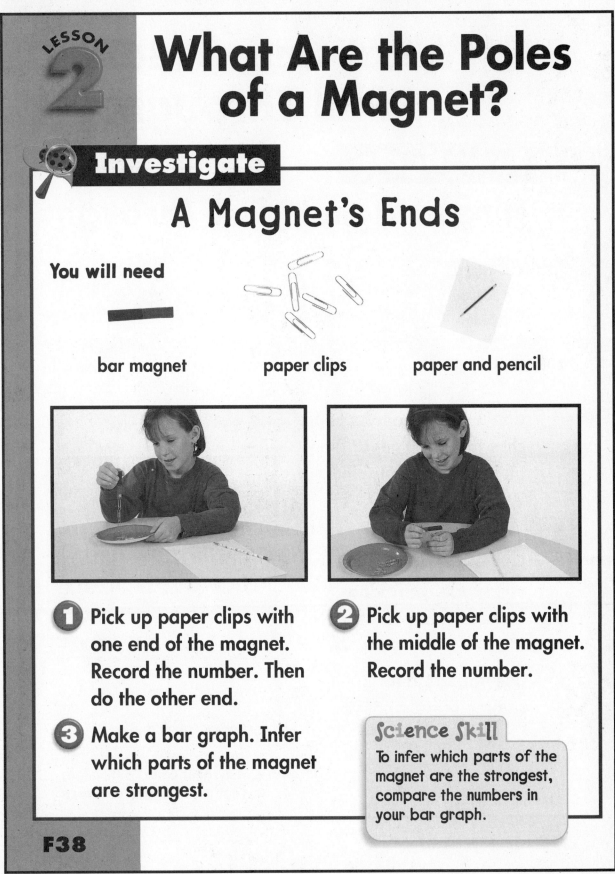

bar magnet   paper clips   paper and pencil

1. Pick up paper clips with one end of the magnet. Record the number. Then do the other end.

2. Pick up paper clips with the middle of the magnet. Record the number.

3. Make a bar graph. Infer which parts of the magnet are strongest.

Science Skill

To infer which parts of the magnet are the strongest, compare the numbers in your bar graph.

F38

Name _____ Date _____

What Can a Magnet Pull Through?

Investigate

Things Magnets Pull Through

You will need

bar magnet   paper clips   different materials

1 Can a magnet attract paper clips through things? Plan an investigation to find out. Write your plan.

2 Follow your plan to investigate your ideas. Record what you observe.

3 Use your data to communicate what you find out.

Science Skill
To investigate what things a magnet can pull through, first make a plan and then try your ideas.

F42

Harcourt

Name _____   Date _____

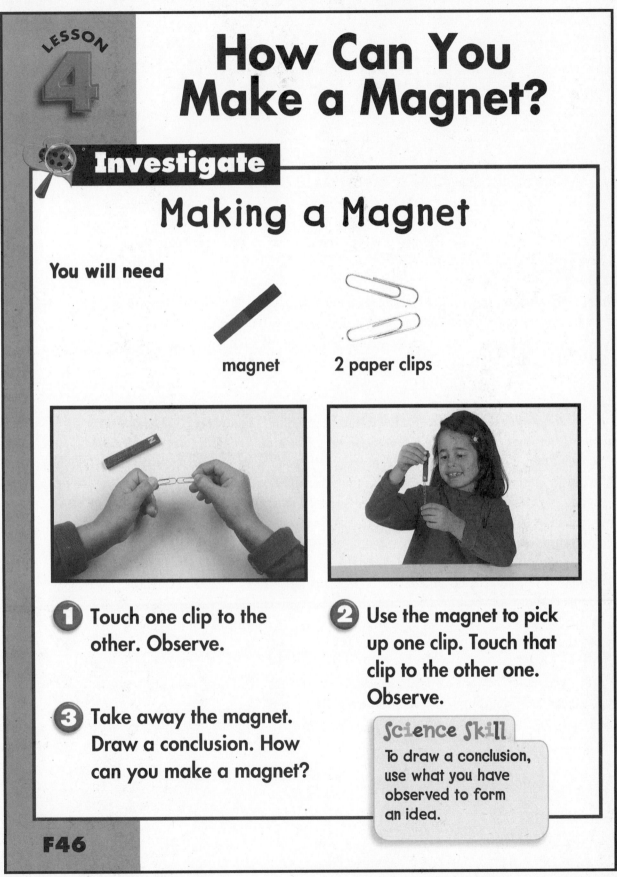

LESSON 4

How Can You Make a Magnet?

Investigate

Making a Magnet

You will need

magnet   2 paper clips

1 Touch one clip to the other. Observe.

2 Use the magnet to pick up one clip. Touch that clip to the other one. Observe.

3 Take away the magnet. Draw a conclusion. How can you make a magnet?

Science Skill
To draw a conclusion, use what you have observed to form an idea.

F46

Harcourt

Participating
in a
School Science Fair

by Barry Van Deman

Science fairs are more than contests for students. They are events that celebrate students' interest and achievement in science. In their first few years of school, students begin to acquire science process skills, such as observing, inferring, measuring, and predicting. Science projects that emphasize these skills are the most appropriate at this stage.

While individual projects at any grade level are fine, whole-class projects or small-group projects are easier to manage and give students experience in working together. In the pages that follow, this guide will focus on small-group and whole-class projects that are completed in the classroom.

The first step to ensure science fair success is to decide on the outcome you want for students and to design projects that will lead them to it. If you want your students to gain skill in observing, inferring, and classifying, you might consider having them do a project that involves collecting objects and sorting them into groups according to observable characteristics. For example, students might collect and sort leaves or observe and classify seashells. Have students record their observations in various ways, such as by drawing, or writing notes or by making a model. These products can be part of a science project display.

The second step to science fair success is to communicate your expectations to students and to their parents or guardians. A letter you can send to parents at the start of the project is included in the following pages. Be sure to keep parents informed as the project progresses.

Finally, keep in mind that working on science fair projects can help your students gain experience in applying science process skills.

Harcourt

A Letter to Family Members

Dear Parent or Guardian,

We will be holding our school science fair on _____.
Participating in a science fair is an enjoyable way for students to apply science process skills that they have been learning at school.

Our project will focus on the following topic:

_____

_____

Our science fair project will emphasize the following science process skill(s):

_____

_____

We will be doing one or more group projects at school. Your child will be part of a project team that will work on a project and display it at the science fair.

Your child can participate by:

_____

_____

Your can aid your child's success by:

☐ helping complete research

☐ visiting _____

☐ sending in the following supplies: _____

_____

_____

I will be sending home more information about our science projects and the science fair. If you have any questions, please contact me at school.

Sincerely,

Harcourt

Ideas for Group Projects

Fuzzy, Hard, and Smooth   Have students find textures in the classroom, at home, and outdoors. Ask them to describe the textures. Groups might display labeled drawings, magazine pictures, photographs, and actual objects.

Shapes All Around Us   Have students find shapes in the classroom, at home, and outdoors. Ask them to identify the shapes. Groups might display labeled pictures and actual objects of various shapes.

Sink or Float   Have students try to float various objects in small tubs of water to see which sink and which float. Groups might display the actual objects, draw them, or show them in a table.

All Kinds of Leaves   Go on a leaf hunt or have students bring leaves they collect near their homes. Have students sort the leaves into groups by characteristics. They might display their groups of leaves by gluing them to poster board and labeling each group by its sorting characteristic.

What Grows from a Seed?   Give each student a dry bean and a paper, plastic, or foam cup filled with potting soil. Have students plant their beans just below the surface of the soil and water them thoroughly (without soaking) each day. Keep the cups near a light source, such as a window. Have students measure, draw, and record their observations daily. Groups might display their plants and charts recording their growth.

What Will a Magnet Pick up (or Attract)?   Give students various metallic and nonmetallic objects and a magnet. Have them test each object to find out if it is attracted to the magnet. For display, group members might draw the objects that are attracted to the magnet on one half of a sheet of poster board and objects that are not attracted on the other half.

How Are Seashells Alike and Different?   Have students sort a collection of seashells into groups by similar characteristics. They might display the unsorted shells along with drawings and descriptions of how they sorted them into groups.

Which Brand of Chocolate Chip Cookies Has the Most Chocolate Chips?   Using at least two brands of cookies, have students carefully break apart cookies and count the number of chocolate chips. Groups can collect the numbers on the chalkboard, and transfer them to poster board for display. They might also want to make graphs using "chocolate chips" made from construction paper.

For additional Science Fair project ideas see pages A1, B1, C1, D1, E1, and F1 in your *Harcourt Science* Teacher's Edition.

Ideas for Displaying Projects

Here are some ideas for displaying student projects in the classroom or at a science fair.

Name _____ Date _____

Science Fair Project Planning

Our Science Project Team

Team Members	What will they do?

Harcourt

Project Results

Our Project

_____
_____
_____
_____

What We Did

_____
_____
_____
_____

What We Found Out

_____
_____
_____
_____

Picture Cards

Card #1
spruce tree

Card #2
spruce cones

Card #3
watermelon slice

Card #4
strawberries

Harcourt

Picture Cards

Card #5
peanuts

Card #6
swan

Card #7
cygnets

Card #8
alligator

Picture Cards

**Card #9
young alligator**

**Card #10
elephant**

**Card #11
elephant calf**

**Card #12
cat**

Harcourt

Picture Cards

Card #13
kitten

Card #14
sea turtle

Card #15
young sea turtle

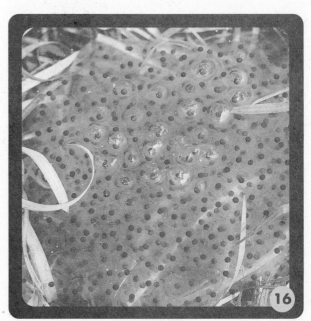

Card #16
frog eggs

Harcourt

Picture Cards

Card #17
tadpole

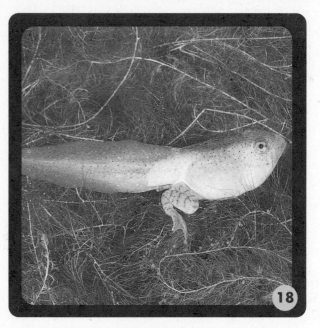

Card #18
tadpole with back legs

Card #19
tadpole with front legs

Card #20
frog

Harcourt

Picture Cards

Card #21
baseball bat

Card #22
straw basket

Card #23
newspapers

Card #24
cotton T-shirt

Harcourt

Picture Cards

Card #25
wooden dresser

Card #26
leather boots

Card #27
wool sweater

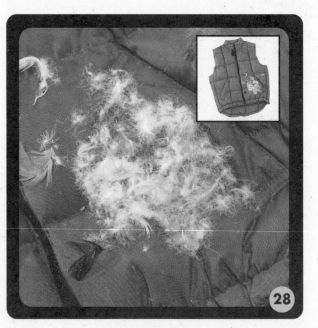

Card #28
goose down vest

Harcourt

Picture Cards

Card #29
leather baseball mitt and ball

Card #30
leather briefcase

Card #31
parrotfish

Card #32
dolphin

Picture Cards

Card #33
shark

Card #34
barracuda

Card #35
turtle

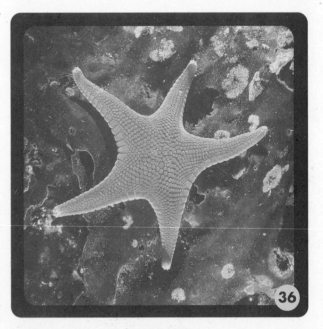

Card #36
starfish

Harcourt

Picture Cards

Card #37
anemone

Card #38
coral

Card #39
grouper

Card #40
sponge

Picture Cards

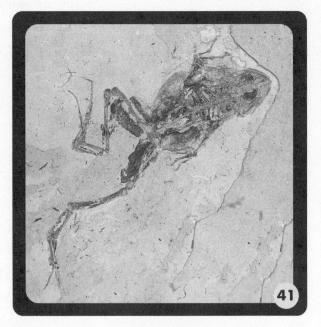

Card #41
frog fossil

Card #42
living frog

Card #43
fish fossil

Card #44
living fish

Harcourt

Picture Cards

**Card #45
clam fossil**

**Card #46
living clam**

**Card #47
conch fossil**

**Card #48
living conch**

Harcourt

UNIT A Activities
for Home or School

Senses Game

Get a box and put in different things. Ask your family or classmates to close their eyes. Have them use touch and hearing to guess each thing.

Nature Walk

Take a nature walk with your class or with family members. Draw or write about what you observe.

Harcourt

A78

Growing and Changing

Look at photos of yourself with a family member. Talk about how you have changed.

Observe a Pet

With an adult, find a pet to observe. Draw or write about the animal.

What does the pet look like?

What does it eat and drink?

Harcourt

A79

Name _____ Date _____

B Activities
for Home or School

What Do Worms Need?

1. Put two kinds of soil and two worms in a covered box.

2. In two hours, check where the worms are.

3. What do the worms need? Talk about what you observe.

Make a Bird Feeder

1. Cut the top off of a plastic jug. Punch holes on both sides.

2. Tie string through the holes.

3. Pour some birdseed inside. Hang outdoors.

4. Observe birds that eat the seeds.

B46

Harcourt

Name _____ Date _____

Rain Forest in a Jar

1. Put pebbles, soil, and plants in a jar.

2. Water the plants. Put the lid on the jar.

3. Put the jar where it gets light but not strong sun.

4. Wait one day. Observe. How is this like a rain forest?

Stems That Store Water

1. Observe the stem tubes, or small dots, on a cut celery stalk.

stem tubes

2. Set the stalk in an empty cup. Put it in the sun until it droops.

3. Add water to the cup. Put it in the refrigerator. The next day, tell what happened and why.

Harcourt

B47

UNIT C Activities
for Home or School

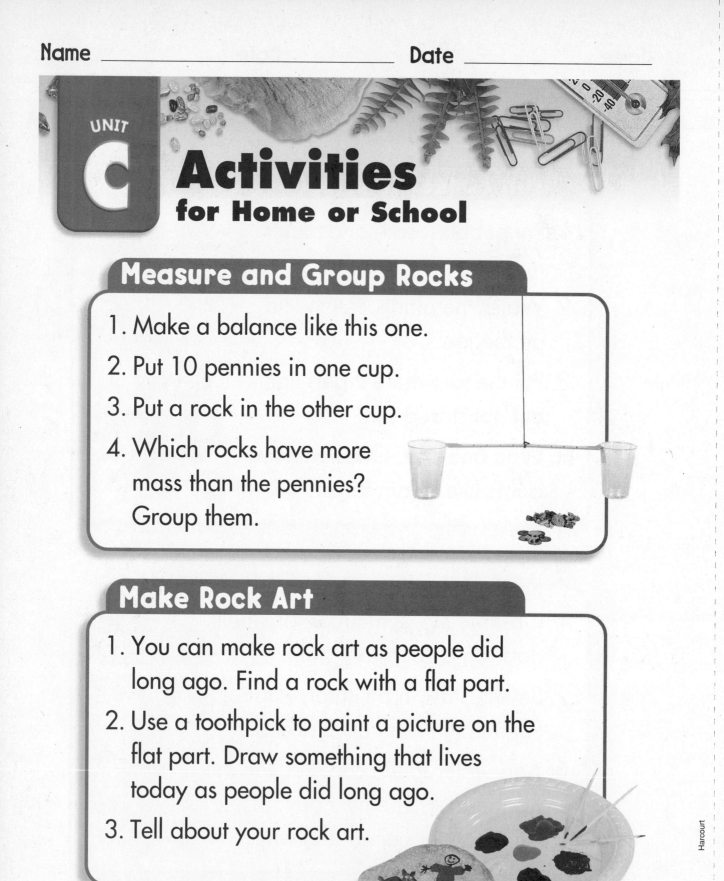

Measure and Group Rocks

1. Make a balance like this one.

2. Put 10 pennies in one cup.

3. Put a rock in the other cup.

4. Which rocks have more mass than the pennies? Group them.

Make Rock Art

1. You can make rock art as people did long ago. Find a rock with a flat part.

2. Use a toothpick to paint a picture on the flat part. Draw something that lives today as people did long ago.

3. Tell about your rock art.

C46

Harcourt

Name _____ Date _____

How Much Air Is in a Breath?

1. Take a big breath.

2. Let it out by blowing into a balloon.

3. With your fingers, hold the end of the balloon closed. Observe how much air you breathed out.

4. Compare balloon breaths to a classmate's or family member's.

Visit a Park

1. With your class or family members, visit a park.

2. Observe how land is being used.

3. Draw a picture that shows what you observed.

4. Share your drawing.

C47

UNIT D Activities
for Home or School

Make a Sail for a Car

Put a paper sail on a toy car. Blow on the sail to make the car move. What could you do to make a better sail? Try your ideas.

Investigate Water Vapor

1. With an adult present, blow into a small plastic bag.

2. Observe the water drops inside. They come from the water vapor in your breath.

3. Put the bag in a freezer for five minutes. Tell what happens.

4. Put the bag in the sun for five minutes. Tell what happens.

D54

Harcourt

Make a Four Seasons Poster

Fold a big sheet of paper into four parts. Label each part for a different season. Add pictures of things you like to do in each season. Talk about how the weather changes.

Find Seasons in a Closet

What clothes do people wear at different times of the year where you live? Brainstorm ideas. Write a list that shows at least two things for each season.

D55

Harcourt

UNIT E

Activities
for Home or School

Make Juice Bars

Change liquid juice into
a solid by making juice pops.

1. Have a family member help you pour
   fruit juice into an ice cube tray.

2. Put a toothpick into each part of the
   tray. *Be careful. Toothpicks are sharp.*

3. Freeze and eat!

Floating Drops

1. Fill a jar with salad oil.

2. Put two or three drops of food coloring
   into the oil. Put the lid on the jar.

3. Tip the jar. What happens to the colored
   drops? Talk about what floats and why.

E54

Harcourt

Listen for Sounds

1. Close your eyes and sit quietly for one minute. Do not speak or move.

2. Listen carefully for sounds.

3. Draw pictures to show the sounds you heard.

4. Compare with a classmate or family member. Which sounds did both of you hear?

Find the Sound

1. All players close their eyes.

2. One player is "it" and rings a bell softly.

3. The other players guess where the sound is coming from.

4. The player who locates "it" makes the next sound.

E55

Harcourt

UNIT F

Activities
for Home or School

Magnetic Kite

1. Cut out a tissue paper kite.
2. Attach thread and a paper clip.
3. Tape the thread's tail to a table.
4. Use the magnet to pick up your kite without touching it.

Magnetic Race-Car Game

1. Draw a road on cardboard.
2. Put two paper clips on the road.
3. Put two magnets under the cardboard. Move the magnets to race your clips.

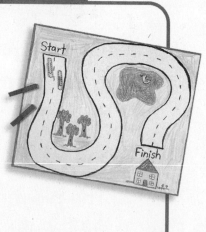

F54

Harcourt

Make a Water Wheel

1. Push toothpicks into the ends of a piece of clay. *Be careful. Toothpicks are sharp.*

2. Push strips cut from a carton into the clay to make a water wheel.

3. Hold the wheel by the toothpicks. Place the wheel under running water.

4. Tell how the water makes the wheel turn.

Marble Fun Slide

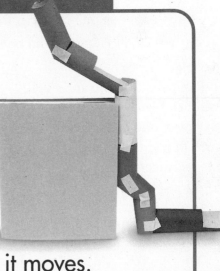

1. Tape together paper towel tubes to make a fun slide.

2. Use books to hold up the tubes.

3. Put a marble at the top, and listen to it race to the bottom. Talk about how it moves.

F55

Harcourt

Vocabulary Activities

The word cards on pages 117–160 contain all the glossary words for Grade 1. The activities that follow suggest ways to use the word cards to:

- increase children's understanding of science terms and concepts.
- help children develop their decoding (phonics, structural analysis, alphabetizing) skills.
- meet the individual needs of your classroom.

Concept Activities

1. Categories

Grouping: Whole class or large group; pairs (Challenge option)

Materials: word cards; paper and pencil (Challenge option)

Present children with groups of word cards that are clearly related in some familiar way. Have children decide what category best describes all three.

Easy: Reverse the procedure. Instead of having children deduce categories, give them the category and help them search through the word cards to find words that fit.

Average: Provide examples by modeling your thinking as you look at a set of words and consider the categories that might describe them. Examples might include:

- reptile, amphibian, insect, mammal (Living Creatures, Animals)
- rock, soil, sand (Things Found on the Ground)

Challenge: Have children work in pairs to come up with their own sets of word cards and categories, which they then try out on other classmates.

"The words are thermometer, ruler, timer."

"Things That Measure Something!"

Harcourt

2. Which One Doesn't Fit?

Grouping: Whole class or large group; pairs (Challenge option)

Materials: word cards; paper and pencil (Challenge option)

This activity is a variation on "Categories." Display sets of word cards in which all but one card have something in common. Identify the category, and ask, "Which one doesn't fit?" Examples might include:

- algae, rock, tadpole: "The category is Living Things. Which one doesn't fit?" (rock)

- roots, leaves, sunlight: "The category is Parts of a Plant. Which one doesn't fit?" (sunlight)

Easy: Limit the activity to 3 word cards, with one that does not fit.

Average: Use 3–4 word cards. As children become comfortable with the activity, increase the number of word cards. You may also wish to use sets of 5 word cards in which 3 cards fit the category and 2 do not.

Challenge: Have pairs of children come up with their own sets of word cards and categories. Ask partners to try their word sets out on their classmates.

---

3. Find the Opposite

Grouping: Whole class or large group

Materials: words cards; drawing materials (options for meeting individual needs)

Before beginning the activity, separate pairs of opposites from the word cards. Choose 6 other word cards that can be used as distracters. To begin, discuss what *opposite* means, using common opposites such as *hard* and *easy*, *tall* and *short*, *day* and *night*.

Easy: Display pairs of opposites. Discuss how the two words in each set differ in meaning. Then have children choose a pair to illustrate, showing graphically how opposite the words are in meaning. Ask children to share their drawings.

Average: Present one word card to children and talk about the word's meaning. Have children find a word in the deck that has an opposite meaning. Discuss how these two words differ in meaning.

Challenge: Have children look through the word cards for a word that they can name an opposite for. Tell them that they can name a word from another word card or another word they know. Children can then illustrate their set of words and present them to the class.

Harcourt

4. Get Off My Back!

Grouping: Whole class or large group; small group (Challenge option)

Materials: word cards, tape; paper and pencil (Challenge option)

Tell children that in this game they must guess a word that is taped on their backs. Select enough words so that every child can have a different word card on his or her back. Be sure to choose words that are easy to describe or talk about. Explain that they will use clues given by classmates to identify the words. Tell children that their word card can be moved from back to front when they have guessed their word. Direct children to mingle, asking one another for hints about their words and giving out hints to others.

Easy: Model giving hints, using a volunteer with a sample word on his or her back. You may also wish to limit the number of words and have partners wear the same word card so they can help each other identify the word.

Average: You may wish to provide time prior to the activity for children to review the words and their meanings. Tell children to think about the hints they will give for each term.

Challenge: Divide children into small groups, taping a word to each child's back. Have group members play a form of Twenty Questions. Tell each child to take a turn asking the group yes-or-no questions about the word, instead of soliciting informative hints from others.

Vocabulary Activities

Harcourt

Decoding Activities

5. Alphabetical Order

Grouping: Individual or Pairs

Materials: word cards, egg timer (optional)

Give children a set of word cards to alphabetize. To add interest to the game, you may wish to pair children and use a three-minute time limit. The first team to alphabetize the words is the winner. Tailor the number of cards and the alphabetizing task to children's' abilities:

Easy: Give children 3 word cards that begin with 3 different letters. Make sure children have access to an alphabet chart.

Average: Give children 5–6 word cards, including some words that begin with the same letter. Elicit or explain that children will need to alphabetize to the second letter.

Challenge: Give children 8–12 words cards, including at least 2 words that begin with the same two letters. Elicit or explain that children will need to alphabetize to the third letter.

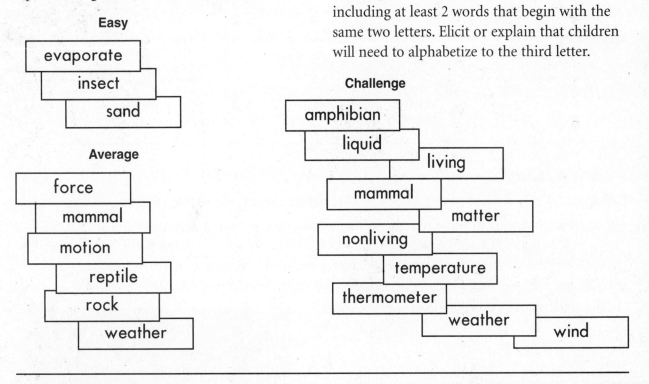

Easy

evaporate
insect
sand

Average

force
mammal
motion
reptile
rock
weather

Challenge

amphibian
liquid
living
mammal
matter
nonliving
temperature
thermometer
weather
wind

6. Sorting Center

Grouping: Individual or Pairs

Materials: word cards, index cards, crayons or colored markers

Give children a set of word cards to sort. Explain that they need to listen to the sounds in the word on each card to sort them. Tailor the number of cards and the sorting task to their abilities:

Easy: On each of three index cards, have children draw a picture of an animal whose name begins with a target consonant sound, such as _lion_, _rabbit_, and _seal_. Have them use the cards as the headings for three sorting columns. Then give children 5–6 cards with words that begin with one of those 3 sounds. Have them sort the cards by beginning sounds, placing each card under the appropriate animal.

Average: Follow the same procedure as described above, but have children focus on ending consonant sounds, such as _lion_, _rabbit_, and _seal_. Then give children 6–8 cards with words that end with one of those 3 sounds. Have them sort the cards by ending sounds, placing each card under the appropriate animal.

Harcourt

Challenge: Give children 8–10 cards with one-syllable words that contain long- or short-vowel sounds. Ask children to sort the cards into groups that contain the same vowel sounds. You may wish to model identifying two cards that contain matching vowel sounds.

Easy	liquid living		reptile rock	sand season
Average	motion season		evaporate insect	mammal reptile soil
Challenge	sand gas hatch	heat seed wheel	float poles	melt stem strength

7. Snap/Clap

Grouping: Whole class or large group   **Materials:** word cards, chalk, chalkboard

Tell children that you are going to hold up two word cards and say the words aloud. They should clap their hands if they hear the same consonant sounds in the two words. They should snap their fingers if the target sounds in the two words are different. Explain that you may focus on beginning, ending, or middle sounds.

On the chalkboard, write the following "equations":

You may wish to provide practice using the following words:

- *cookie/king* and *noodle/fasten* for beginning consonant sounds.
- *bridge/music* and *bottom/room* for ending consonant sounds.
- *pitcher/dazzle* and *dinner/tunnel* for medial consonant sounds.

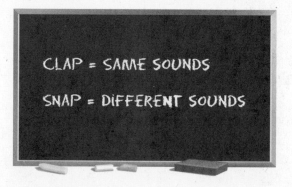

Easy: Use beginning consonant sounds. You may wish to use the following Grade 1 words:

poles/push (clap)   desert/living (snap)   motion/melt, (clap)
larva/lake (clap)   gas/repel (snap)   winter/wind (clap)

Average: Use ending consonant sounds. You may wish to use the following Grade 1 words:

seed/wind (clap)   hatch/shelter (snap)   change/spring (snap)
rock/lake (clap)   pull/mammal (clap)   push/zigzag (snap)

Challenge: Use medial consonant sounds. You may wish to use the following Grade 1 words:

desert/season (snap)   ocean/motion (clap)   mammal/matter (snap)
weather/solid (snap)   pupa/repel (clap)   prism/river (snap)

Harcourt

8. Bingo

Grouping: Whole class or large group

Materials: word cards, medium-sized bag, 8 1/2 × 11 paper, pencil, coins or other flat markers

Have children divide their paper into a 3 × 3 grid. Have children print a different letter of the alphabet in each square. Put various word cards in a bag, all starting with different letters. As a word card is pulled out and the word slowly pronounced and repeated, children should decide if the beginning sound matches a letter on their card and put a marker on that letter. As soon as a child has a row filled down, across, or diagonally, he or she should raise a hand and be declared the winner of that round.

Easy: Provide children with the nine letters to write on the grid. Allow them to decide the placement of the letters on the grid. Act as the caller, pulling words out of the bag and pronouncing them for children, emphasizing the beginning sound.

Average: Direct children to choose any letter of the alphabet to print in each square of the grid, making sure they use nine different letters. You may wish to remind children that few words begin with letters such as *x* and *q*. Act as the caller, pulling words out of the bag and pronouncing them for children, emphasizing the beginning sound.

Challenge: Have children take turns being the "caller."

---

9. Match the Word, Picture, Letter

Grouping: Whole class or group

Materials: word cards, magazine pictures, scissors, 3 × 5 index cards, markers

Look through magazines to cut out pictures that illustrate a few (3–4) glossary words that begin with different consonants. Create letter cards for the beginning consonant sound in each word, writing the letters on individual index cards.

Easy: Have children focus on one word card with its related letter card and picture. Have children look through magazines for pictures of other items that begin with the same sound.

Average: Make a random arrangement of letter cards, pictures, and word cards. Let children take turns arranging the cards so that each word card is in a row with its picture and beginning letter/letter sound.

Challenge: Have children focus on words that begin with a digraph. You may wish to suggest such words as *shelter*, *thermometer*, and *change*.

10. Syllable Sort

Grouping: Large or small group

Materials: shoe boxes, word cards, labels, tape, marker, access to a dictionary, paper and pencil, extra index cards and markers

Have children sort the word cards according to the number of syllables they hear. Prior to the activity, label or have children label four shoe boxes as follows:

- Words with 1 Syllable
- Words with 2 Syllables
- Words with 3 Syllables
- Words with 4 or More Syllables.

Easy: Limit the activity to words with one or two syllables. Have pairs of children practice clapping out the number of syllables in some familiar words (book, ruler, pencil, chalk) before they begin sorting the word cards.

Average: Have children begin the sort with the words they are most certain about. If they are not sure how many syllables are in a word (such as *temperature*), they should consult a glossary or dictionary.

Challenge: When they have sorted all the word cards, children can tally up the number of words in each box to determine which box has the most words. Tell them to use their science textbook to look for other words with the same number of syllables. Have them put these words on index cards, and place them in the appropriate boxes.

Vocabulary Activities

Harcourt

nonliving

senses

roots

living

senses

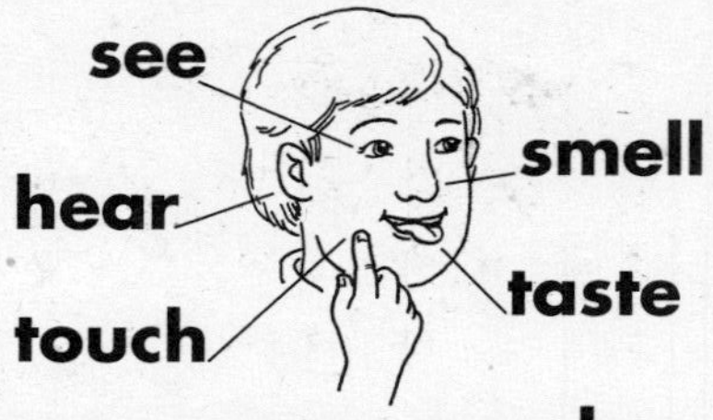

You use your **senses** to see, hear, smell, touch, and taste.

see
smell
taste
hear
touch

nonliving

Rocks and air are **nonliving** things.

living

People are **living** things.

roots

roots

Water is taken into a plant through its **roots**.

Harcourt

Vocabulary Cards

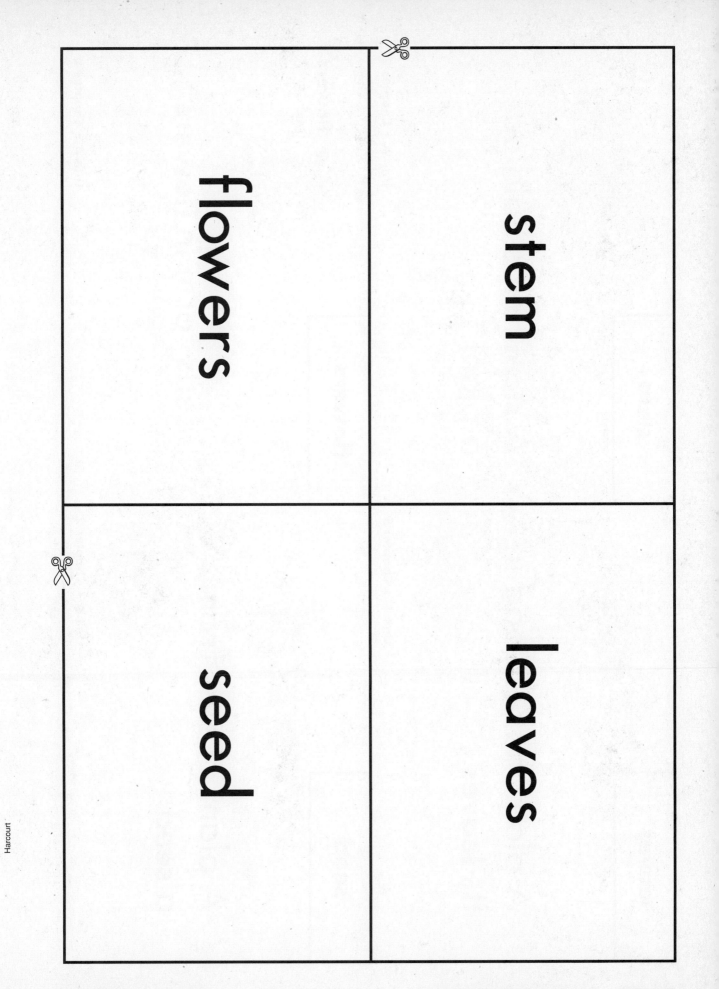

flowers

stem

seed

leaves

Vocabulary Cards

Teaching Resources • TR119

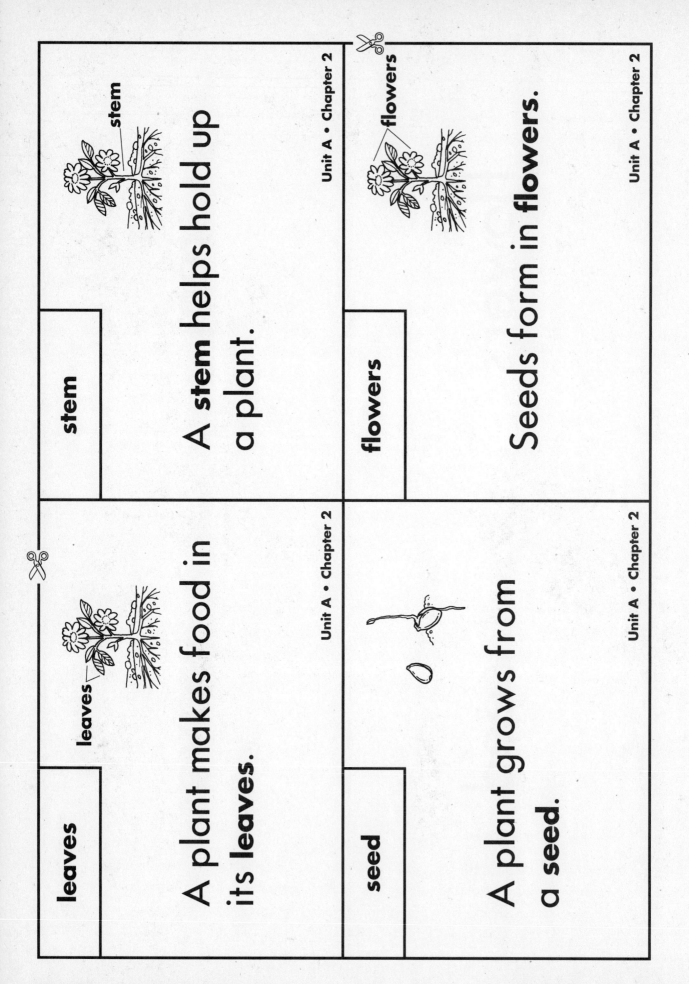

stem

A **stem** helps hold up
a plant.

flowers

Seeds form in **flowers.**

leaves

A plant makes food in
its **leaves.**

seed

A plant grows from
a **seed.**

Harcourt

Vocabulary Cards

seed coat

gills

sunlight

mammal

Harcourt

seed coat

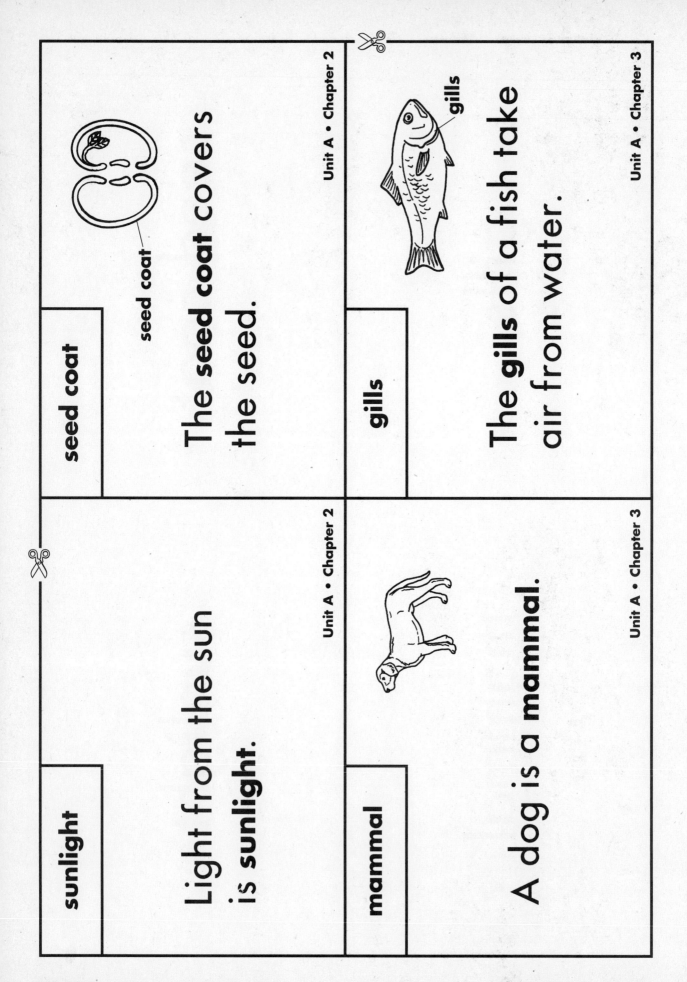

seed coat

The **seed coat** covers
the seed.

gills

gills

The **gills** of a fish take
air from water.

sunlight

Light from the sun
is **sunlight**.

mammal

A dog is a **mammal**.

Vocabulary Cards

Harcourt

insect

reptile

hatch

amphibian

Harcourt

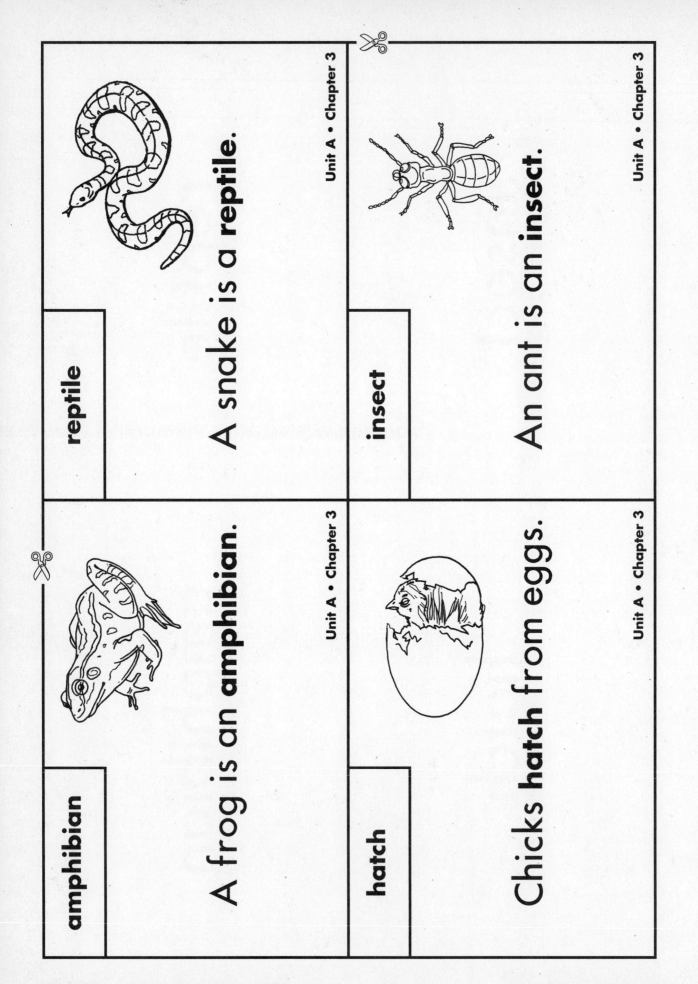

reptile

A snake is a **reptile**.

insect

An ant is an **insect**.

amphibian

A frog is an **amphibian**.

hatch

Chicks **hatch** from eggs.

Vocabulary Cards

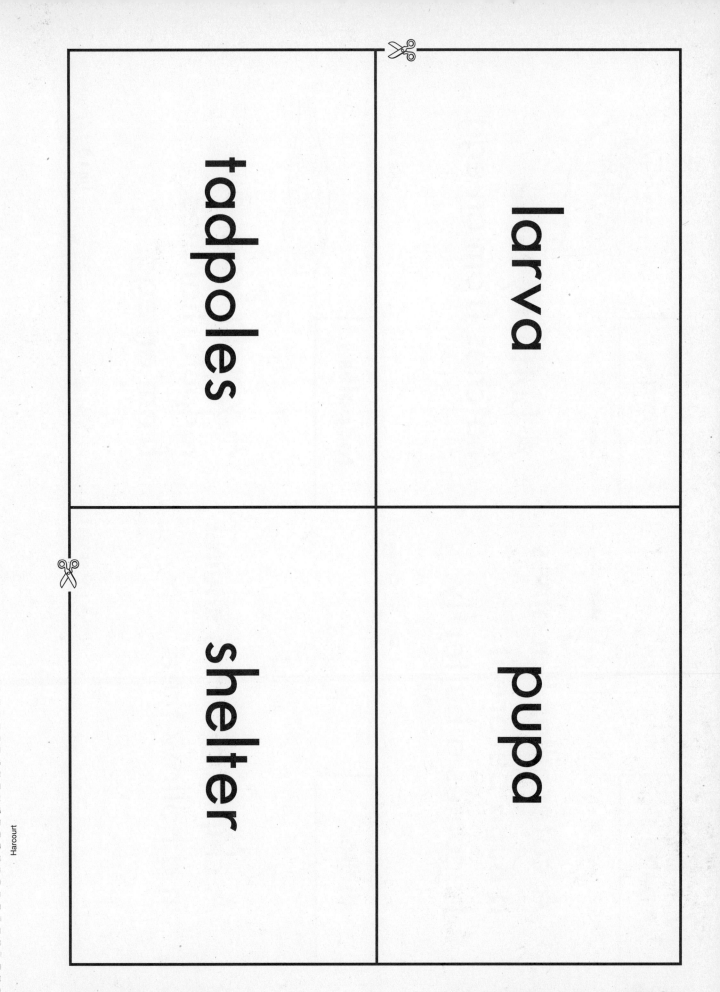

larva

tadpoles

pupa

shelter

Harcourt

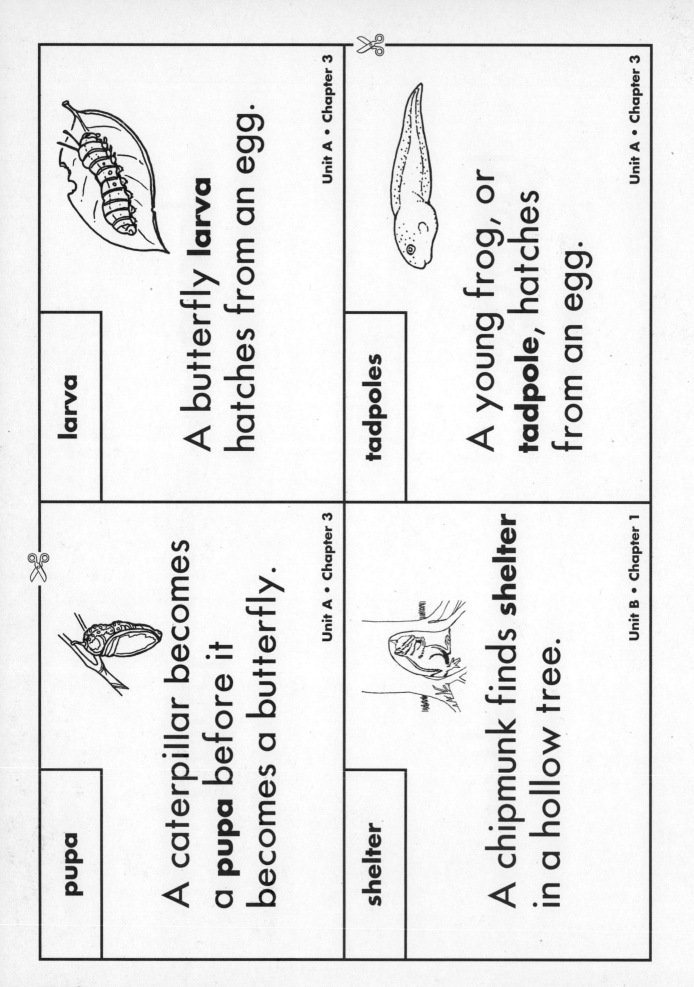

larva

A butterfly **larva** hatches from an egg.

tadpoles

A young frog, or **tadpole**, hatches from an egg.

pupa

A caterpillar becomes a **pupa** before it becomes a butterfly.

shelter

A chipmunk finds **shelter** in a hollow tree.

Vocabulary Cards

Harcourt

product

enrich

forest

pollen

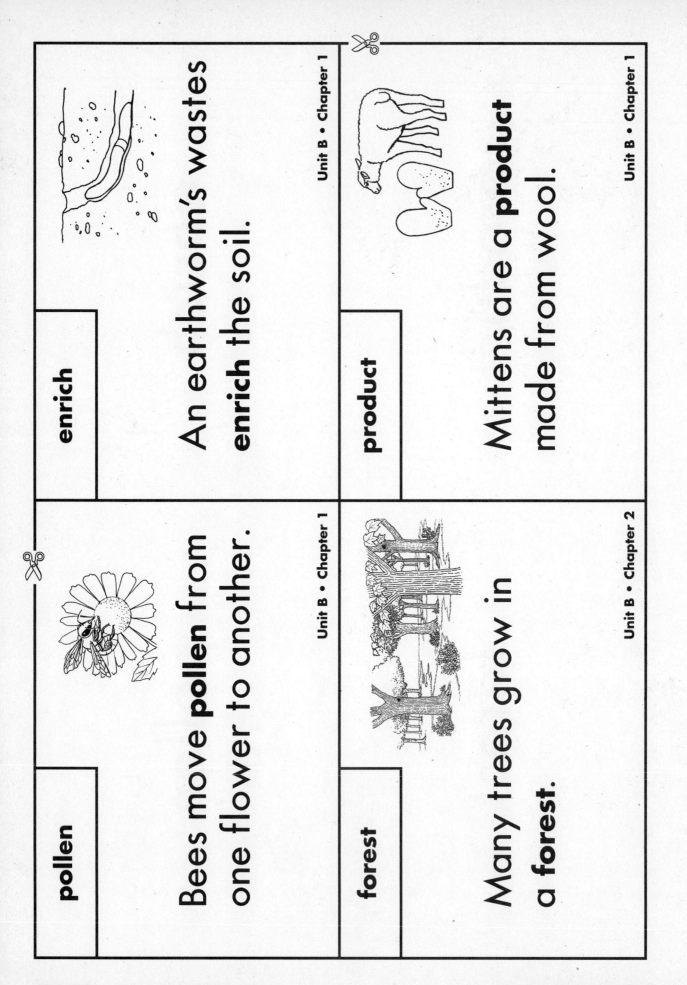

enrich

An earthworm's wastes **enrich** the soil.

product

Mittens are a **product** made from wool.

pollen

Bees move **pollen** from one flower to another.

forest

Many trees grow in a **forest**.

Harcourt

Vocabulary Cards

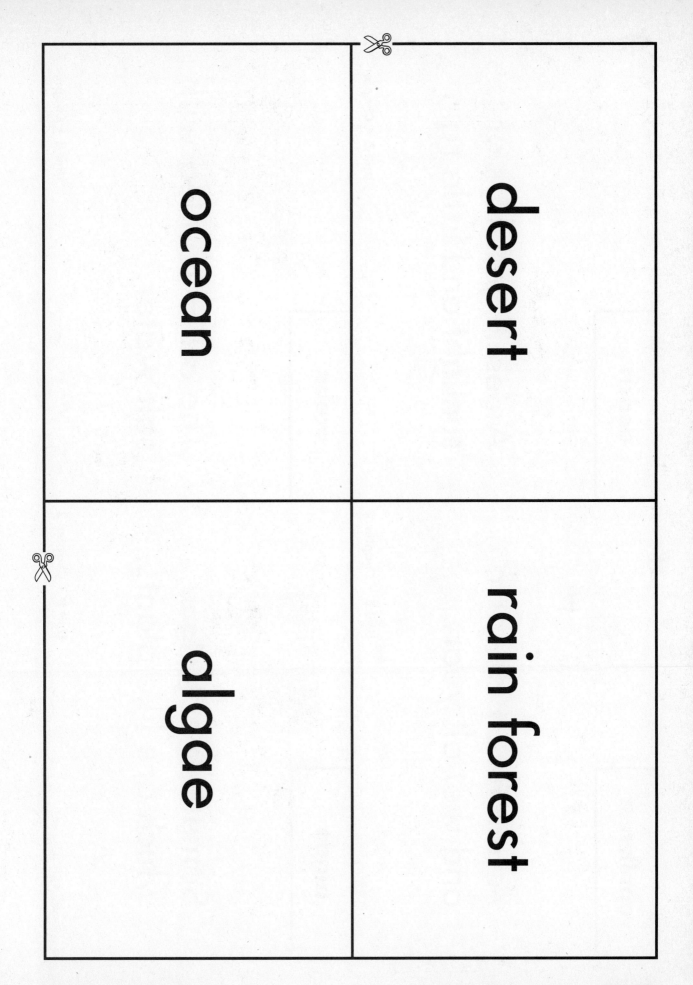

ocean

desert

algae

rain forest

Harcourt

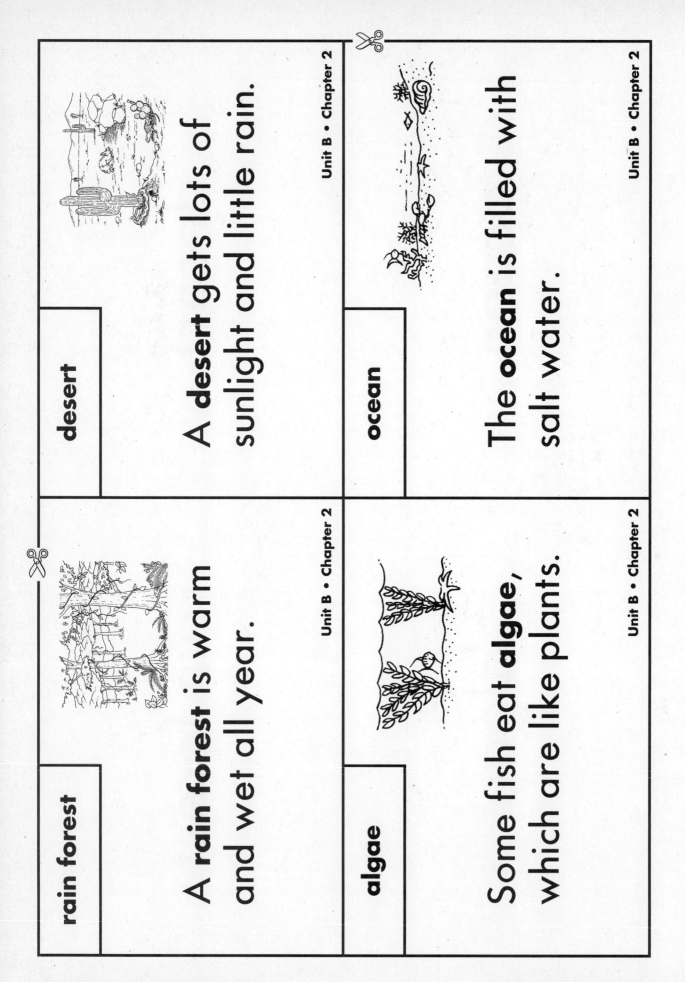

desert

A **desert** gets lots of sunlight and little rain.

ocean

The **ocean** is filled with salt water.

rain forest

A **rain forest** is warm and wet all year.

algae

Some fish eat **algae**, which are like plants.

Vocabulary Cards

fossil

sand

extinct

rock

Harcourt

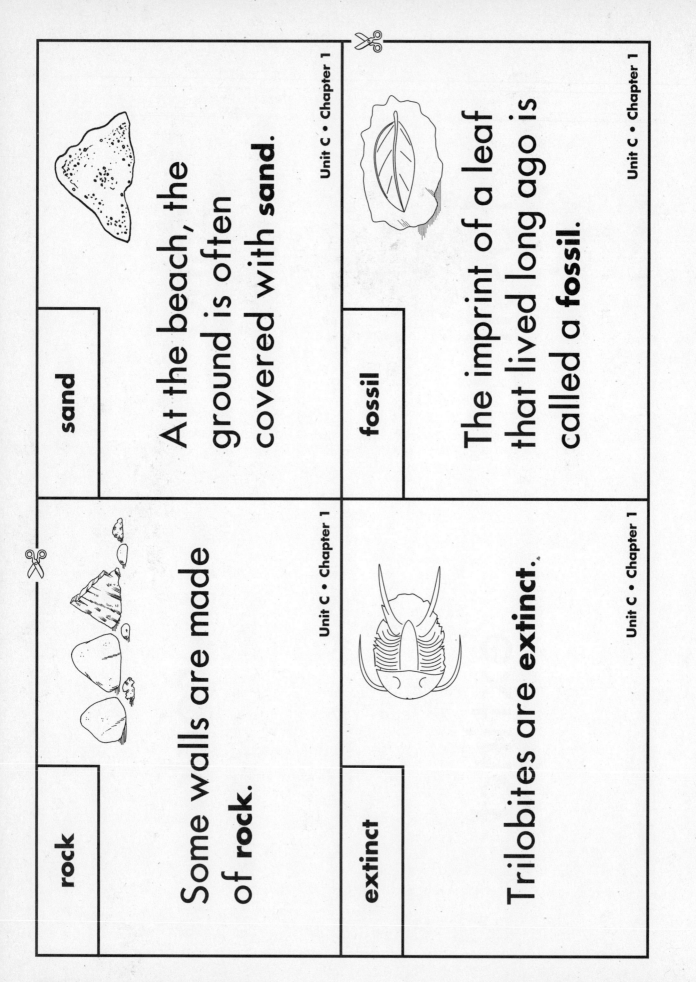

sand

At the beach, the ground is often covered with **sand**.

fossil

The imprint of a leaf that lived long ago is called a **fossil**.

rock

Some walls are made of **rock**.

extinct

Trilobites are **extinct**.

Vocabulary Cards

natural resource

air

mineral

fresh water

Harcourt

Vocabulary Cards

natural resource	Water, land, and air are examples of a **natural resource.**

air	You breathe **air.** It's all around you.

mineral	Garnet is a **mineral.**

fresh water	Water in most lakes, streams, and rivers is **fresh water.**

Vocabulary Cards

Harcourt

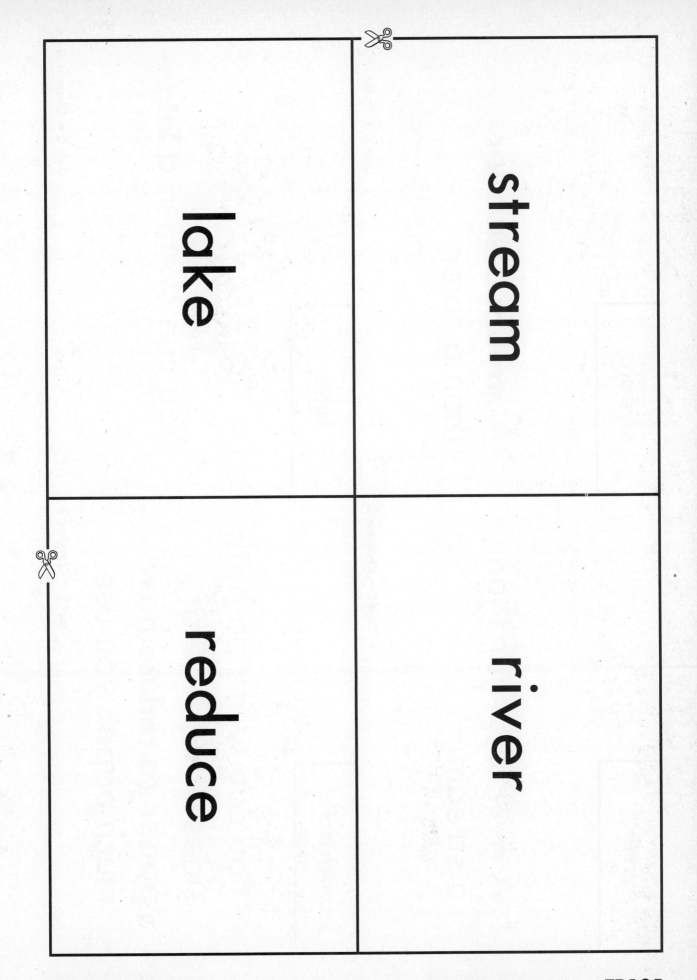

lake

stream

reduce

river

stream

A **stream** is smaller than a river.

lake

You can swim in a **lake**.

river

A **river** is larger than a stream.

reduce

You can write on both sides of a piece of paper to **reduce** how much paper you use.

Harcourt

Vocabulary Cards

weather

reuse

temperature

recycle

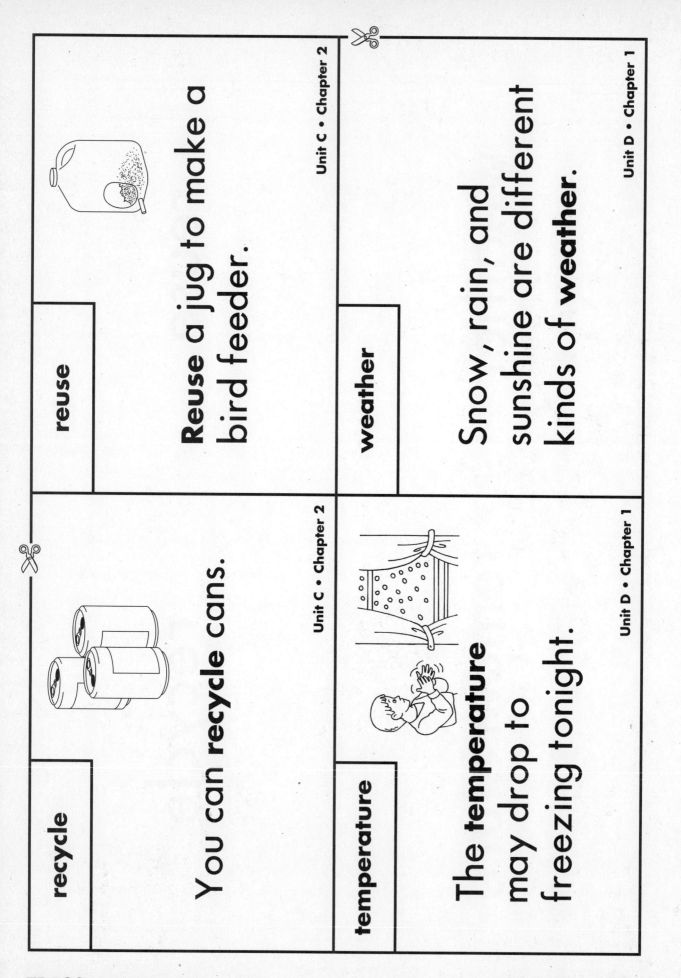

reuse

Reuse a jug to make a bird feeder.

weather

Snow, rain, and sunshine are different kinds of **weather**.

recycle

You can **recycle** cans.

temperature

The **temperature** may drop to freezing tonight.

Vocabulary Cards

Harcourt

thermometer

water cycle

wind

evaporate

Harcourt

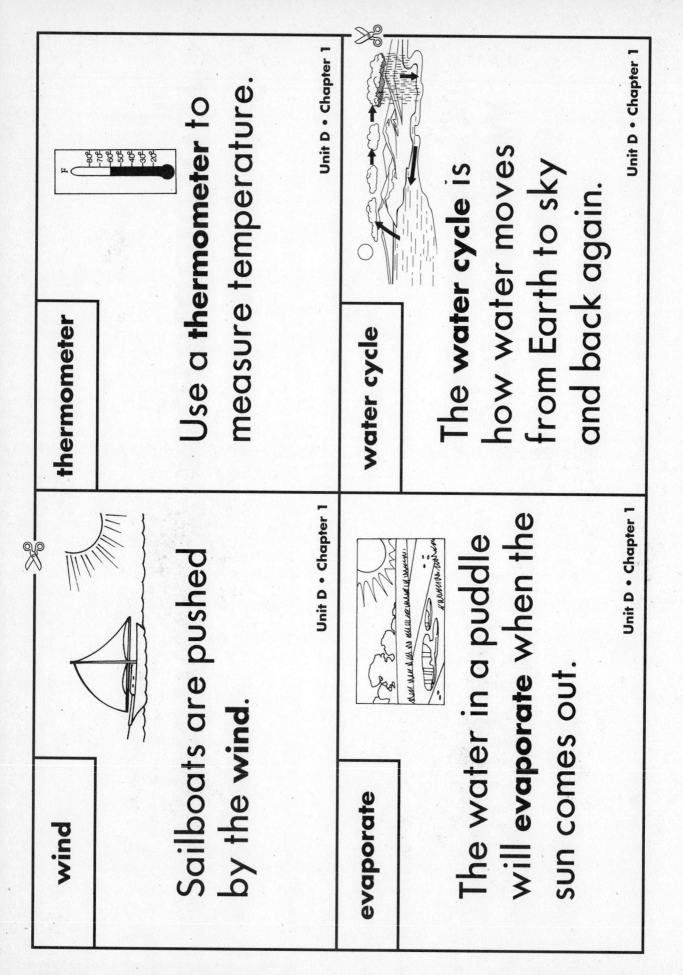

thermometer

Use a **thermometer** to measure temperature.

water cycle

The **water cycle** is how water moves from Earth to sky and back again.

wind

Sailboats are pushed by the **wind**.

evaporate

The water in a puddle will **evaporate** when the sun comes out.

Vocabulary Cards

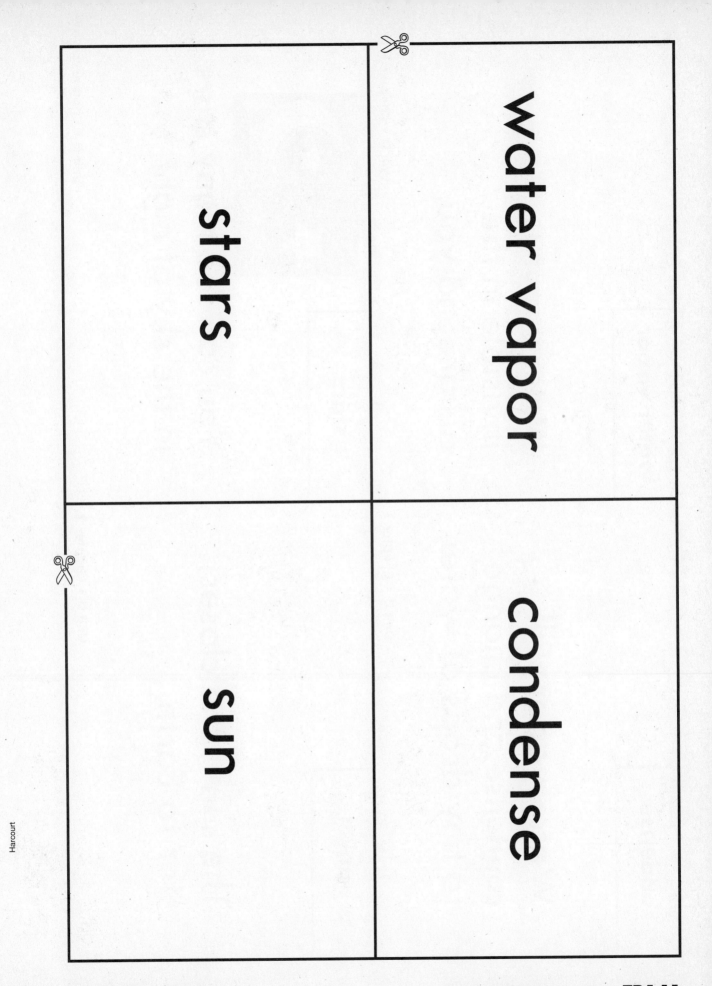

water vapor

stars

condense

sun

water vapor

Water vapor is invisible in the air around you.

condense

Water vapor will **condense** and change to tiny drops of water.

stars

You can see many **stars** in the sky at night.

sun

The **sun** is the closest star to Earth.

Vocabulary Cards

Harcourt

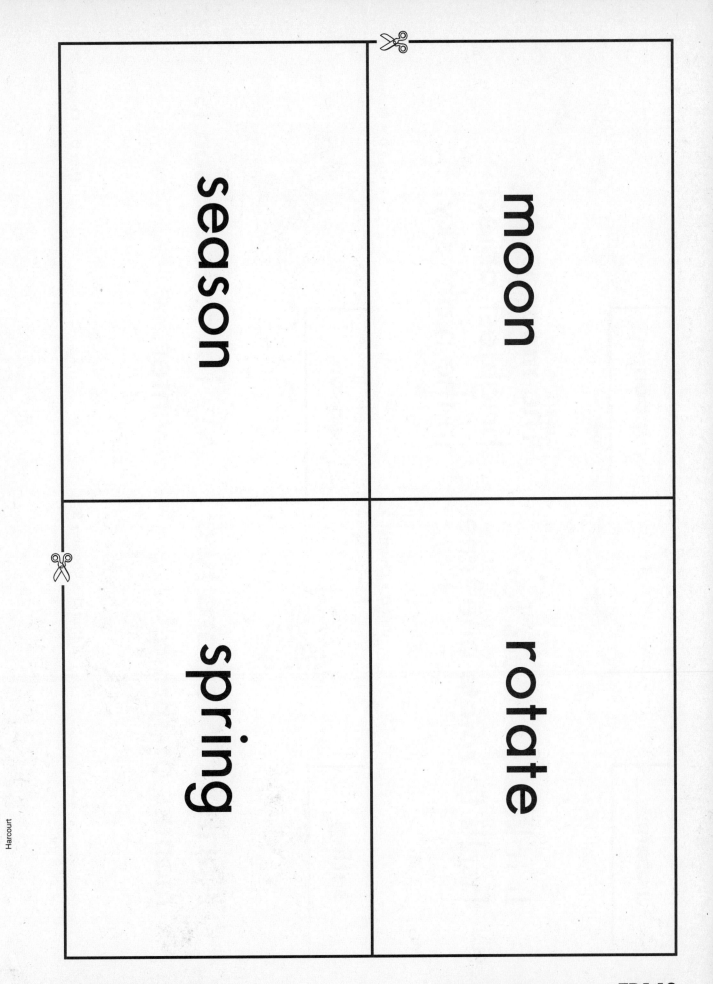

season

moon

spring

rotate

Harcourt

Vocabulary Cards

Teaching Resources • TR143

rotate

It takes 24 hours for Earth to **rotate** one time.

Unit D • Chapter 2

moon

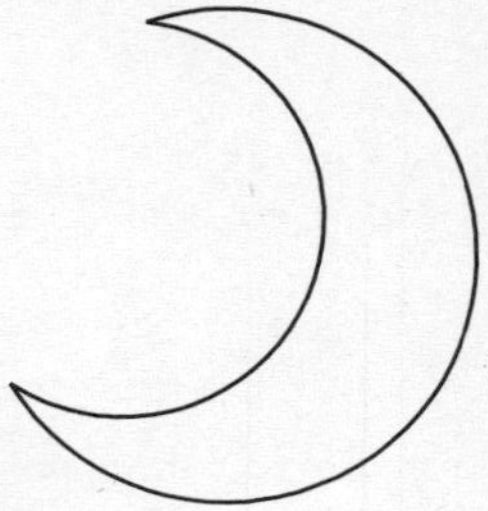

The **moon** is the brightest object in the night sky.

Unit D • Chapter 2

spring

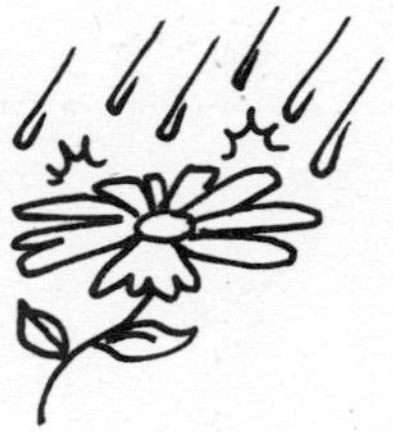

April and May are two months of **spring**.

Unit D • Chapter 2

season

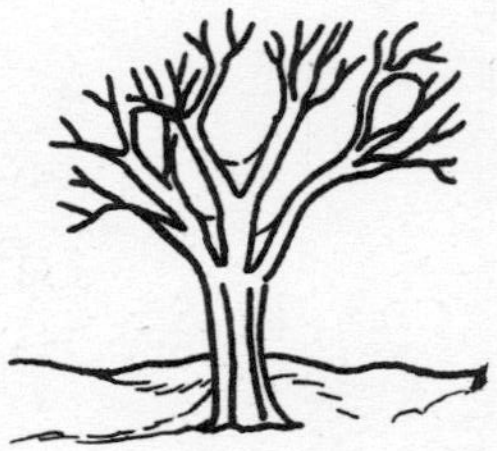

My favorite **season** is winter.

Unit D • Chapter 2

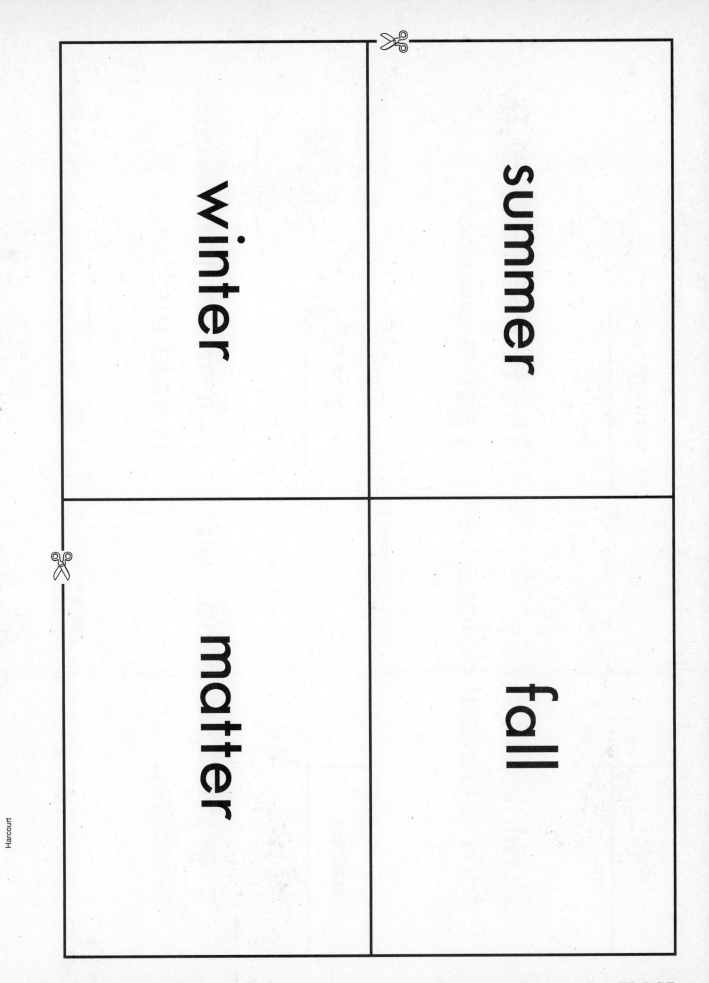

summer

winter

fall

matter

Harcourt

fall

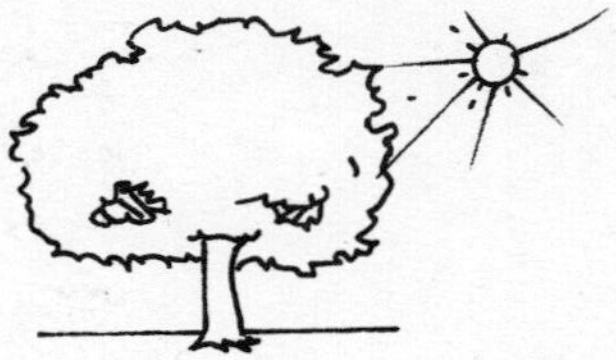

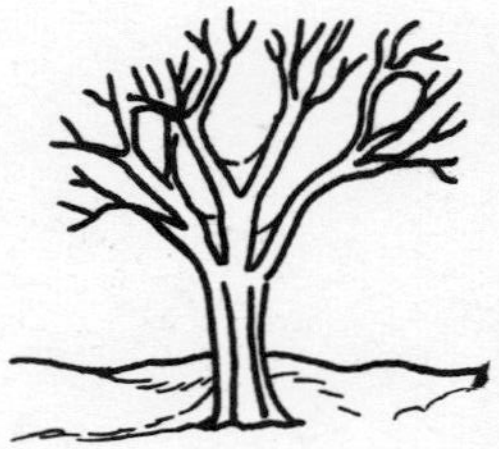

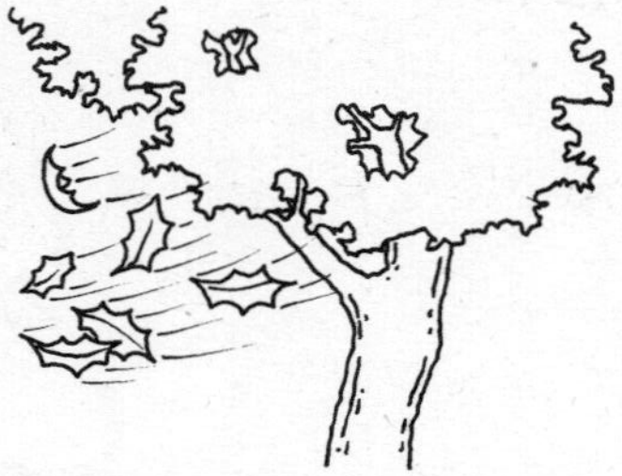

In **fall** leaves may turn different colors.

Unit D • Chapter 2

summer

The hottest time of the year is **summer**.

Unit D • Chapter 2

matter

Everything around you is **matter**.

Unit E • Chapter 1

winter

In many places, **winter** is cold and snowy.

Unit D • Chapter 2

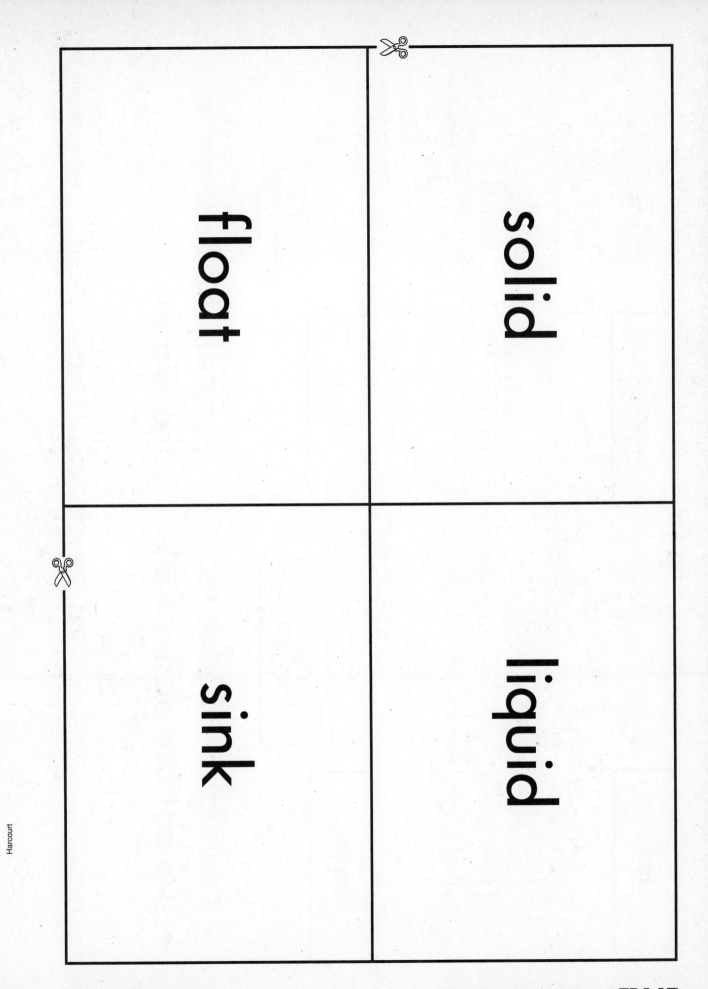

float

solid

sink

liquid

Harcourt

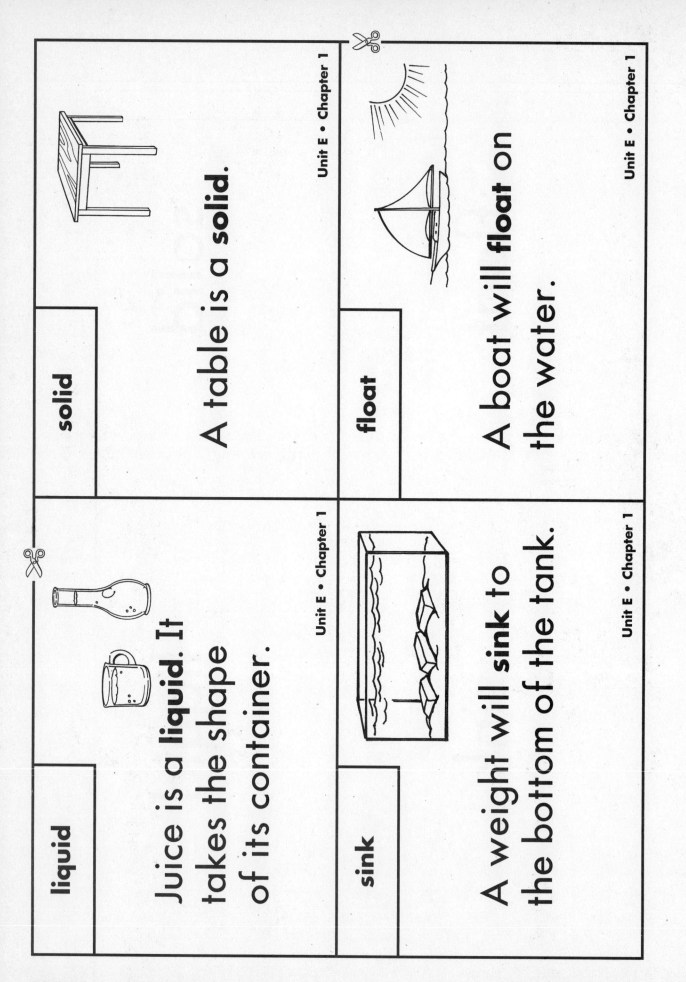

solid

A table is a **solid**.

float

A boat will **float** on the water.

liquid

Juice is a **liquid**. It takes the shape of its container.

sink

A weight will **sink** to the bottom of the tank.

Vocabulary Cards

Harcourt

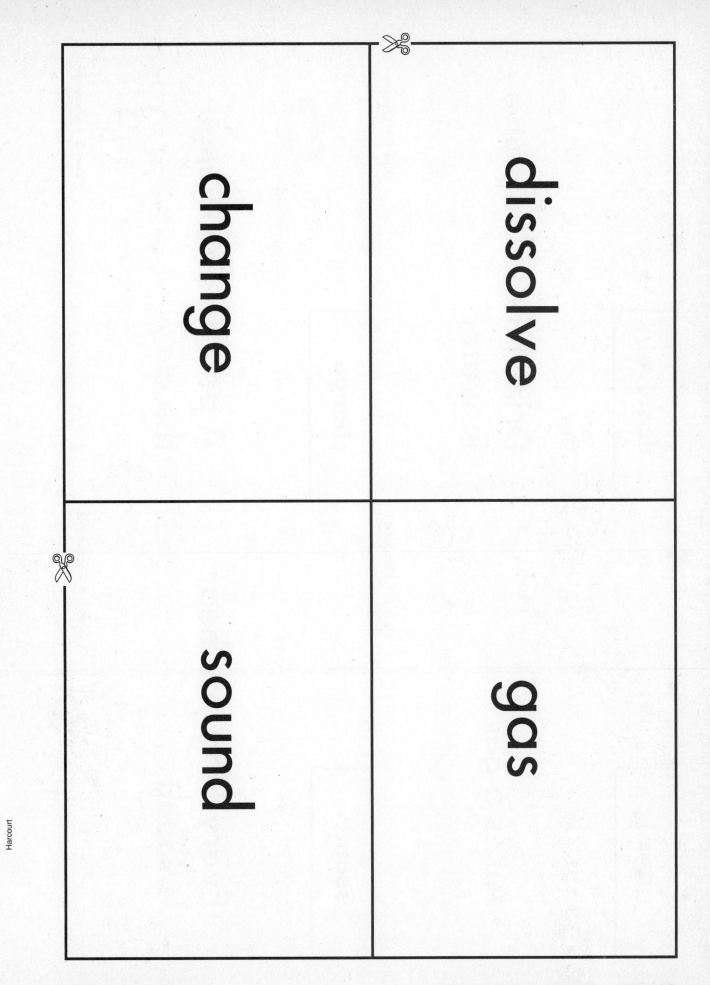

change

dissolve

sound

gas

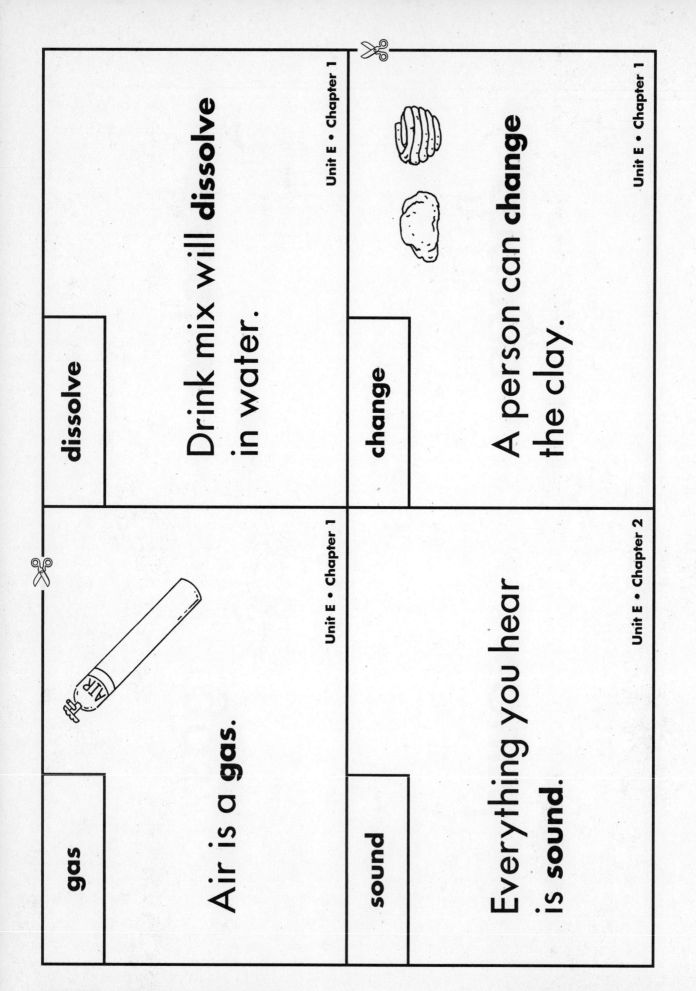

dissolve

Drink mix will **dissolve** in water.

change

A person can **change** the clay.

gas

Air is a **gas**.

sound

Everything you hear is **sound**.

Vocabulary Cards

musical instrument

vibrate

force

pitch

Harcourt

vibrate

The ball inside a whistle will **vibrate** when it is blown.

musical instrument

A **musical instrument** is used to make music.

pitch

The **pitch** of a sound is how high or low the sound is.

force

A push is a **force**.

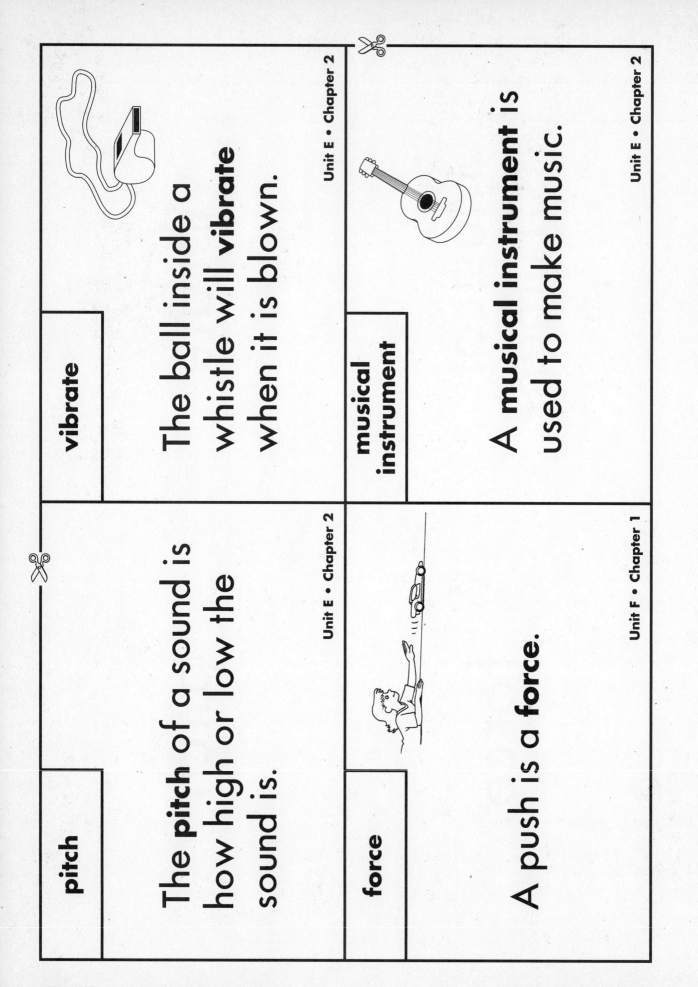

Vocabulary Cards

Harcourt

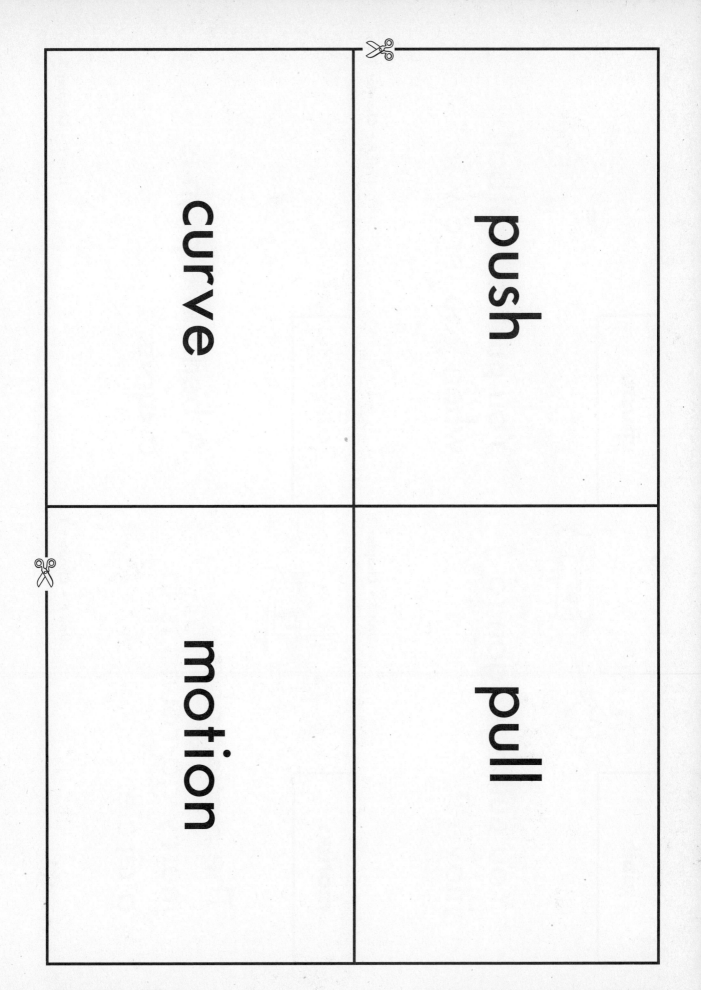

curve

push

motion

pull

Vocabulary Cards

push

You **push** a football when you throw it.

curve

A bend in a path is a **curve**.

pull

You **pull** a wagon to move it.

motion

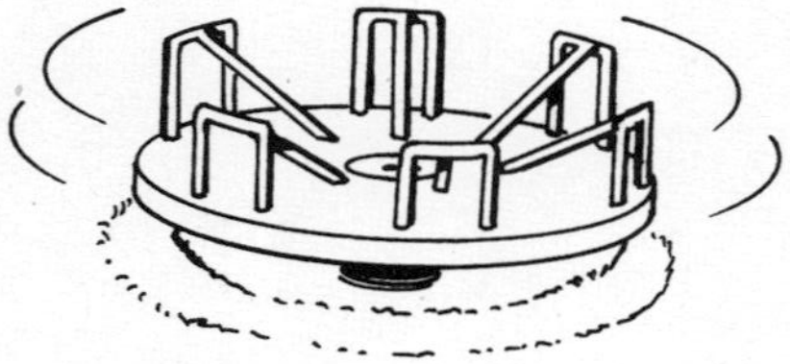

The **motion** of a merry-go-round is in a circle.

Vocabulary Cards

Harcourt

friction

speed

wheel

surface

Vocabulary Cards

Teaching Resources • TR155

speed

Speed is how quickly or slowly something moves.

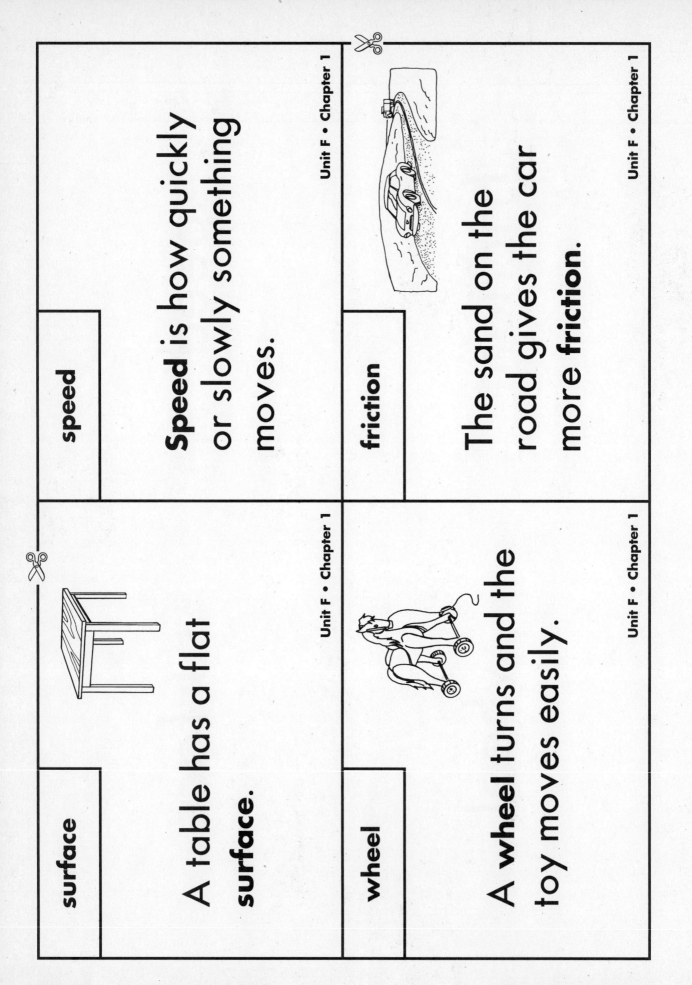

friction

The sand on the road gives the car more **friction**.

surface

A table has a flat **surface**.

wheel

A **wheel** turns and the toy moves easily.

Harcourt

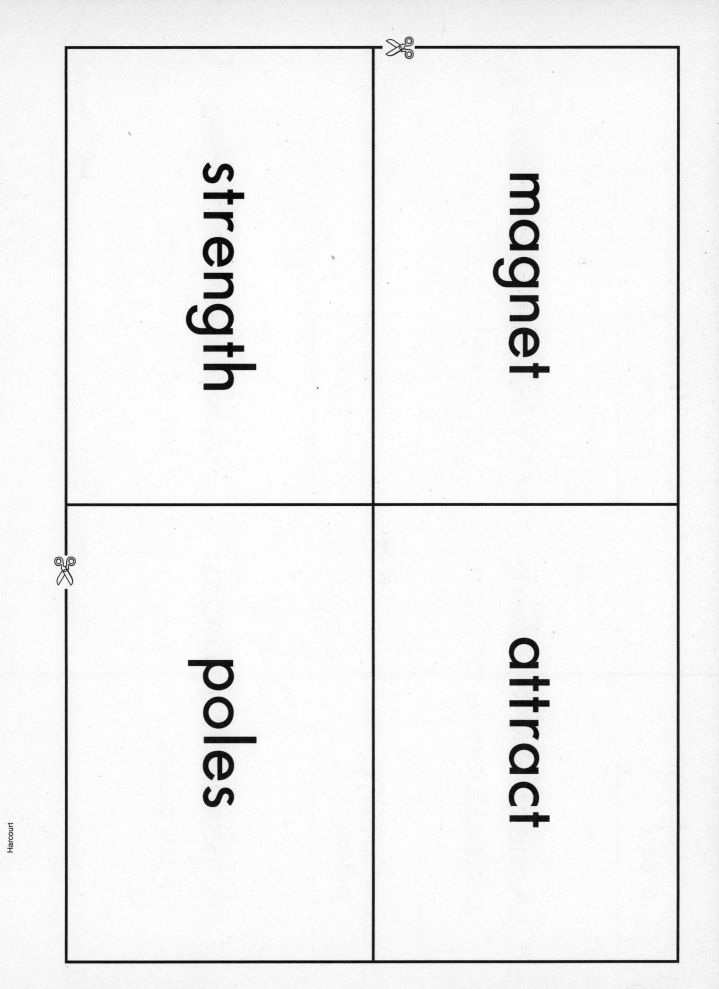

strength

magnet

poles

attract

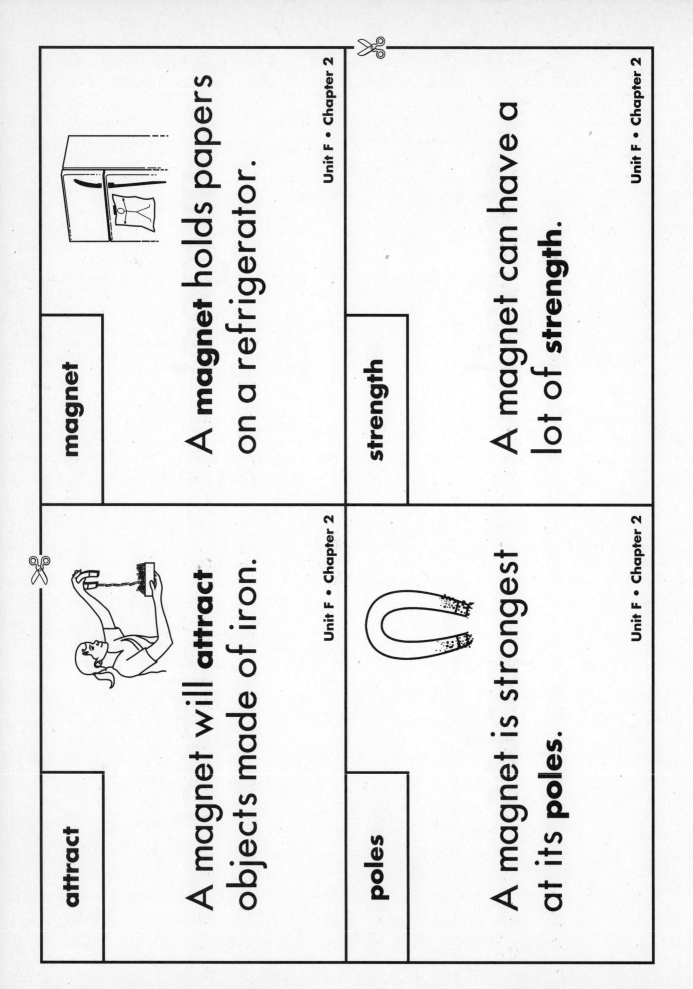

magnet

A **magnet** holds papers on a refrigerator.

strength

A magnet can have a lot of **strength**.

attract

A magnet will **attract** objects made of iron.

poles

A magnet is strongest at its **poles**.

Vocabulary Cards

Harcourt

magnetize

repel

magnetic
force

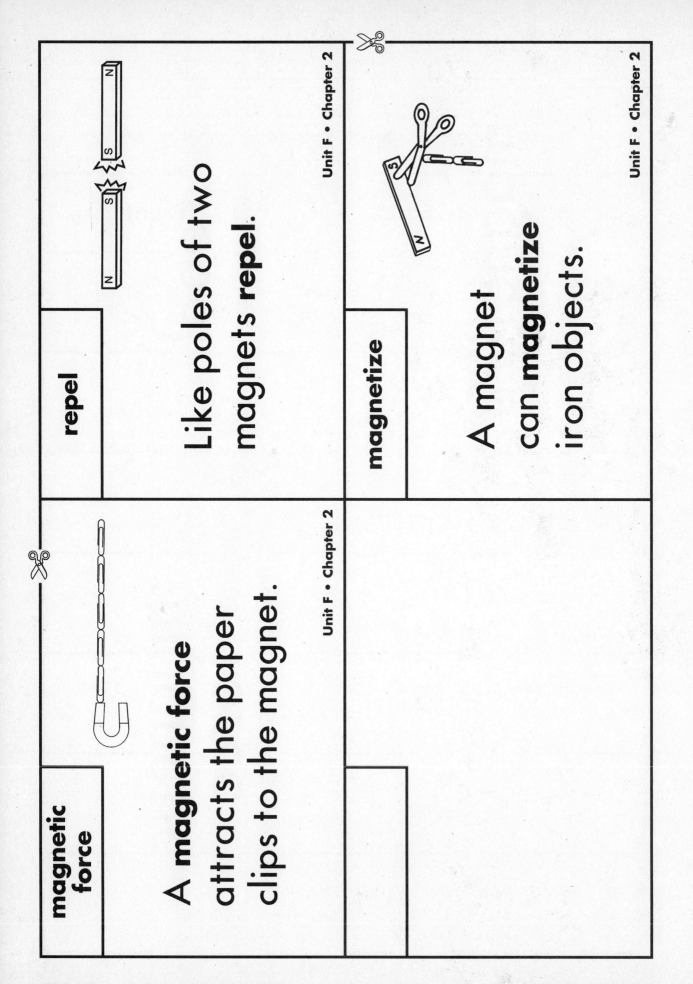

repel

Like poles of two magnets **repel**.

magnetize

A magnet can **magnetize** iron objects.

magnetic force

A **magnetic force** attracts the paper clips to the magnet.

Vocabulary Cards

Harcourt

Animals and Their Young

Animal	Same	Different
cats	Both have ears. Both are orange.	One is big. One is small.

Harcourt

Name _____ Date _____

Rocks

Red			

Harcourt

Name _____ Date _____

Things I Saw Outdoors	
animals	
plants	
water	
land	
soil	

Harcourt

Name _____   Date _____

Inside

F°   C°
                      — 40
100 —
                      — 20
80 —
60 —
                      — 0
40 —
20 —
                      — -20
0 —
-20 —
                      — -40
-40 —

Outside

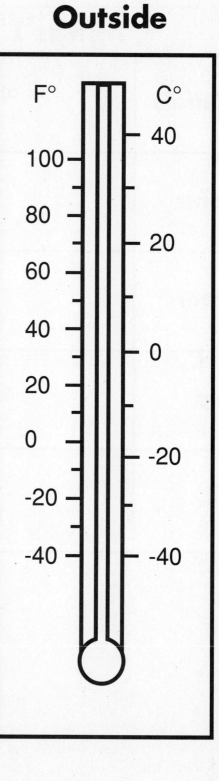

F°   C°
                      — 40
100 —
                      — 20
80 —
60 —
                      — 0
40 —
20 —
                      — -20
0 —
-20 —
                      — -40
-40 —

Harcourt

Temperature

Color	Start	30 minutes later
white		
black		
red		
yellow		

Name _____ Date _____

Solids in Water

	My hypothesis		My results	
	Will dissolve	Will not dissolve	Did dissolve	Did not dissolve
salt				
sand				
rocks				
baking soda				

Use with page E16.

Harcourt

Name _____ Date _____

What a Magnet Can Do

Object	Pulls	Does not pull

Harcourt

Project Plan

What We Want to Find Out

1.

How We Can Find Out

2.

What We Need to Do

3.
Materials

How We Can Share Information

4.

Harcourt

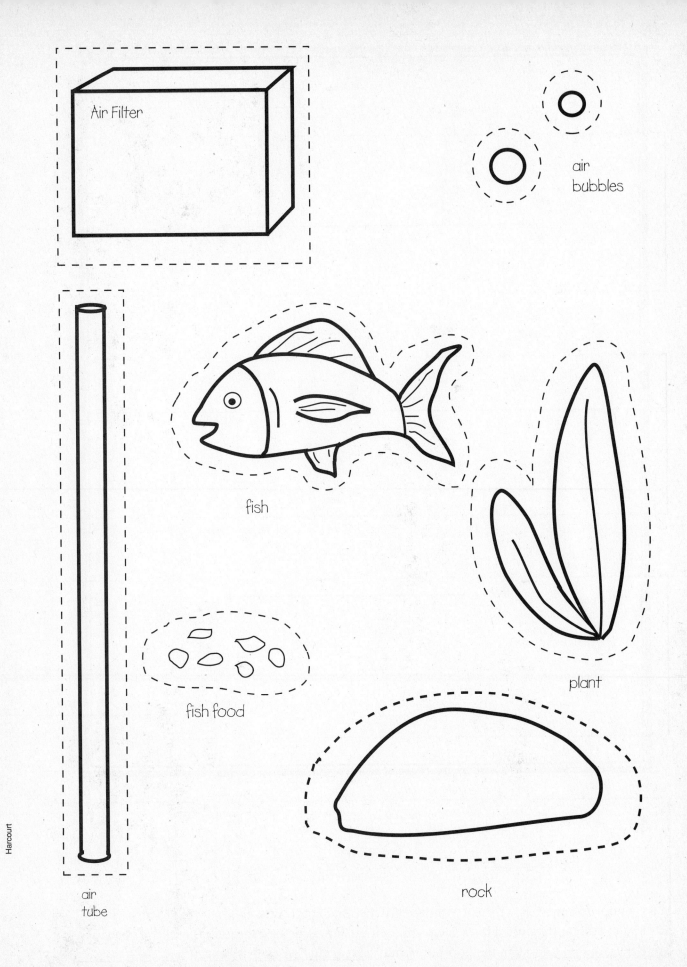

Air Filter

air
bubbles

fish

plant

fish food

rock

air
tube

Harcourt

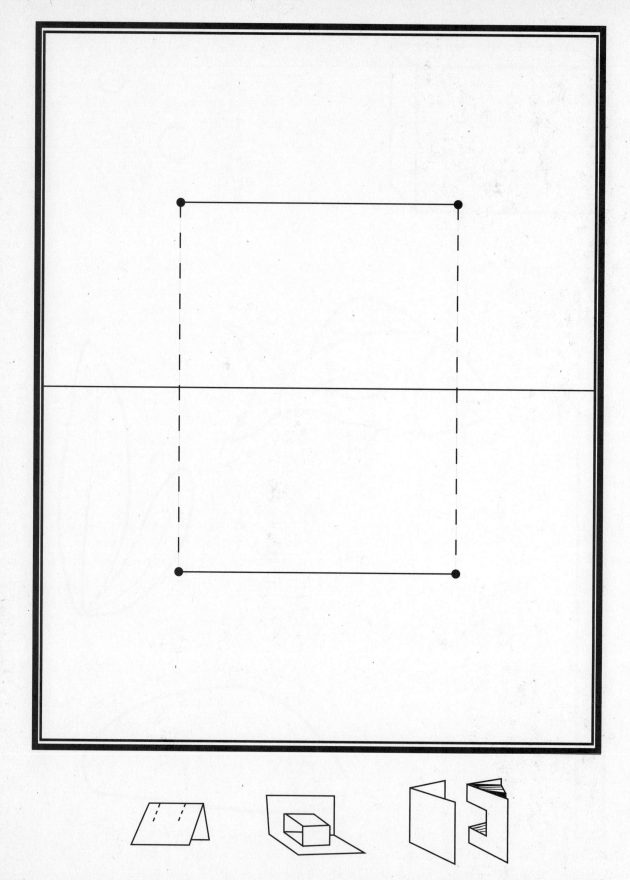

Make a pop-up card. Copy the pattern on construction paper. Have children fold their paper in half and cut along the dotted lines. Help children push the cut area through the fold. Then crease along the solid lines to form the pop-box. Children can glue on an extra sheet.

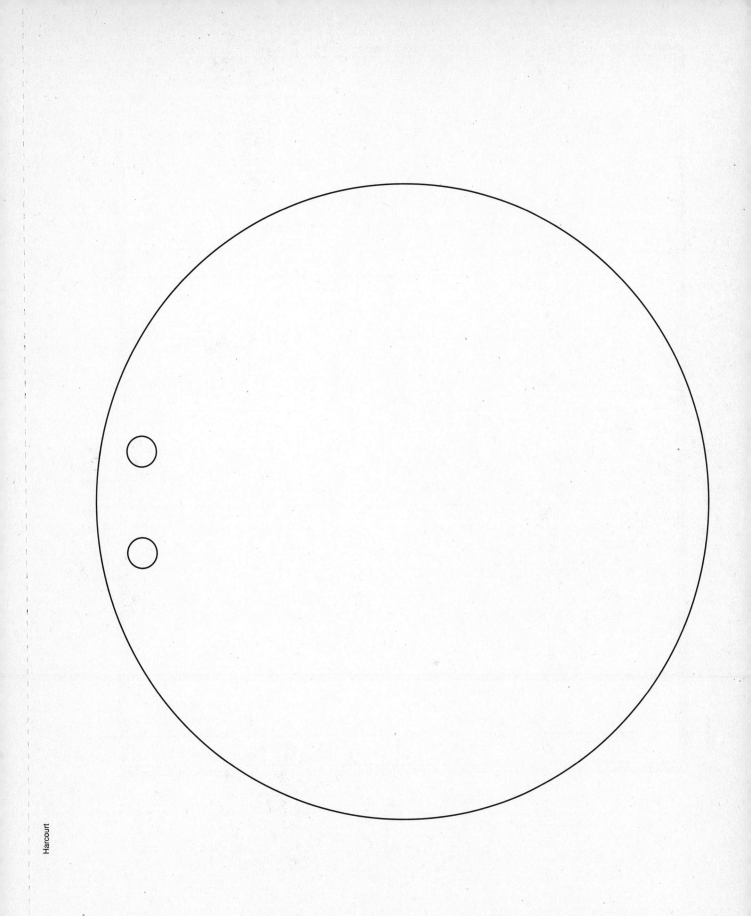

Use with TE page D55.

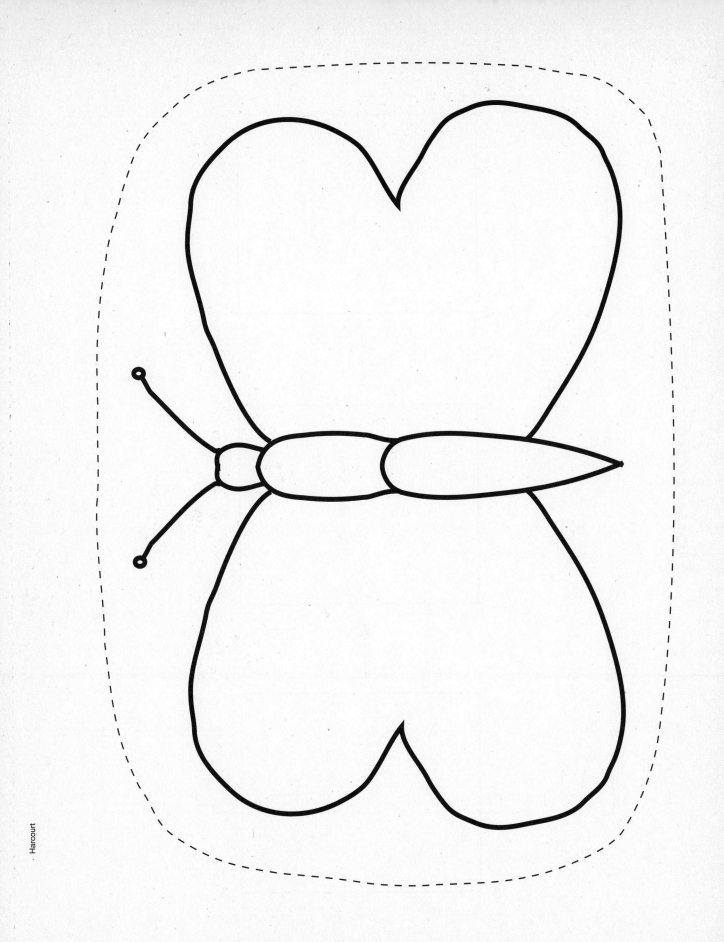

Flowchart

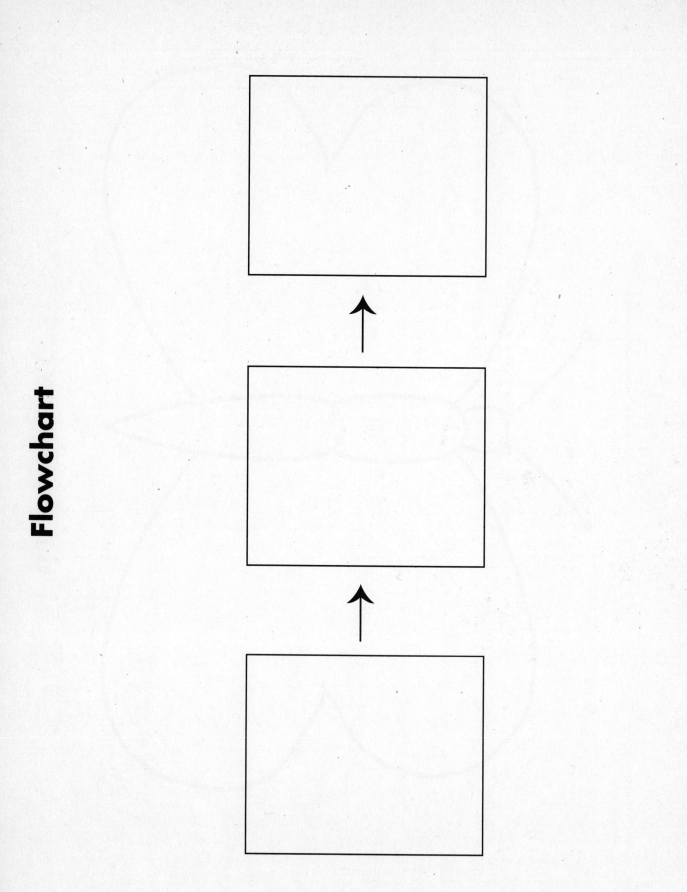

Harcourt

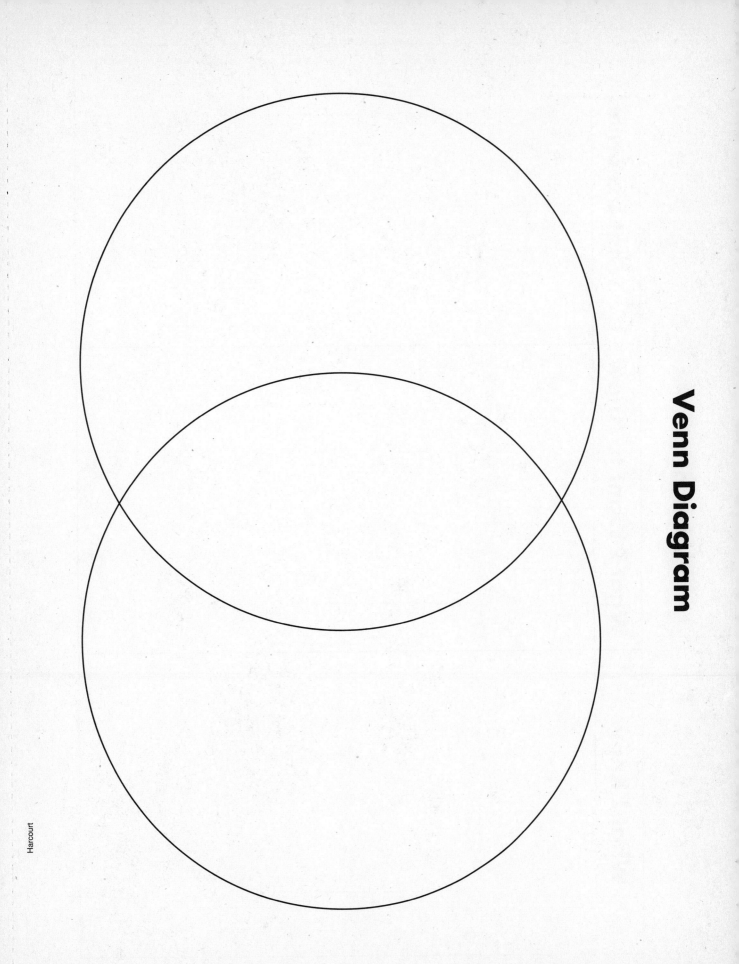

Venn Diagram

K-W-L Chart

What I Know	What I Want to Know	What I Learned

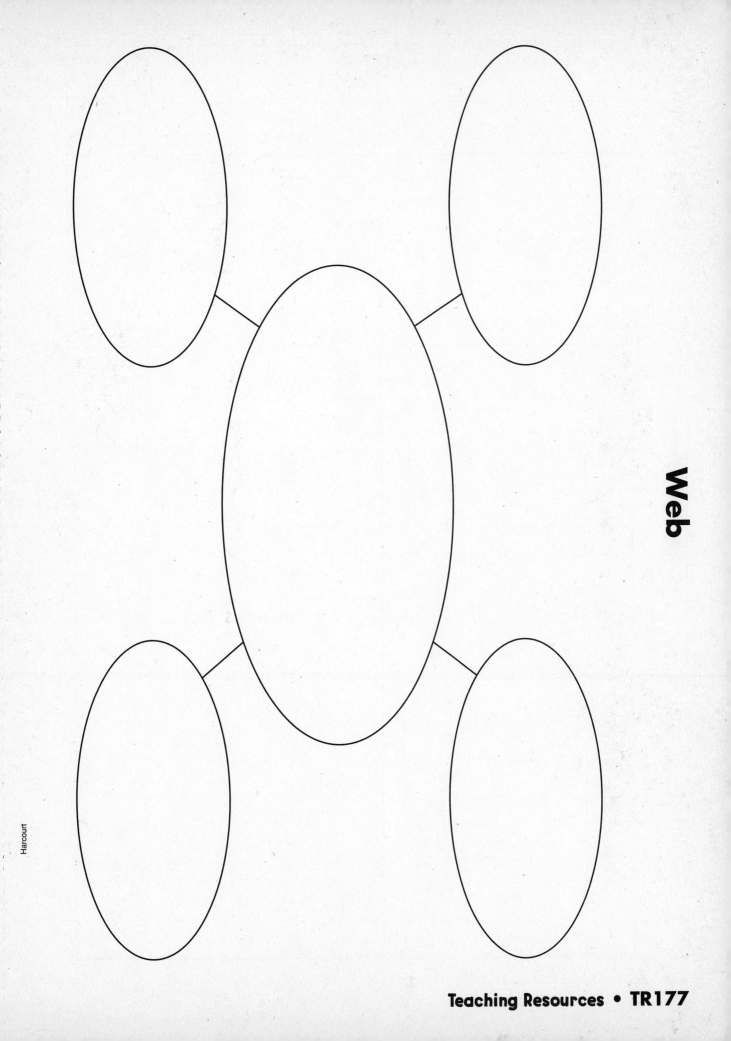

Web

Chart

Harcourt

1-inch graph grid

Writing Models

The writing models on the following pages show examples of writing for different purposes. Children can consult these as they complete various writing assignments described in the *Harcourt Science* Teacher's Edition. You may wish to distribute copies of the writing models to children or display them on an overhead transparency.

Write to Inform TR182
Write to Describe TR183
Write a How-to TR184
Write a Story TR185
Write a Letter TR186

Writing in Science

You can write **information sentences** to tell about something. They should answer the questions *Who? What? Where?* and *When?*

A bird is an animal that has feathers and wings. Mother birds lay eggs. Some birds live on land. Some live near water. Some birds fly south for the winter.

Writing in Science

Model: Paragraph That Describes

You can write a **paragraph that describes** to tell about something you have seen. Use words that tell how the thing looks, sounds, tastes, smells, or feels.

> Our class visited the seashore last week. The waves were noisy, and the air smelled fishy. We saw big brown seagulls. I brought back some soft white sand.

Writing in Science

You can write **how-to sentences** to tell how to make or do something. Make sure you tell the steps in the right order. Words like *first, next,* and *last* will make it easier for the reader to understand.

It is easy to see how cold changes water. All you need is a cup, some water, and a freezer. First, put the water in the cup. Next, put the cup in the freezer. Leave it there for a few hours. Last, take the cup out of the freezer. The water has turned to ice.

Harcourt

Writing in Science

Model: Story

You can write a **story** about different kinds of characters. Remember to tell what happens to them in the beginning, middle, and end of the story.

Little Froggy hatched from an egg. At first, he was a tiny tadpole swimming in the pond. Then he started to change little by little. He grew legs and lost his tail. At last, he climbed out of the water. Now he was a frog!

Harcourt

Writing in Science

You can write a **letter** to tell someone about something you have done or seen. Remember to start with a greeting to the person you are writing to. Be sure to sign the letter at the end.

Dear Mom and Dad,

Grandpa and I hiked to a lake yesterday. We went swimming. The fresh water is a lot different than the ocean water back home. It doesn't taste salty. Grandpa says that the water comes from melted snow in the mountains.

Love,
Adam

Harcourt